Selected Poems:

Kenneth Slessor

Study notes for Common Module:
Texts and Human Experiences 2019–2023 HSC

Bruce Pattinson &
Suzan Pattinson

A
FIVE SENSES
PUBLICATION

Five Senses Education Pty Ltd
2/195 Prospect Highway
Seven Hills 2147
New South Wales
Australia

First Published 2018

Pattinson, Bruce & Pattinson, Suzan
Top Notes – Kenneth Slessor
ISBN 978-1-76032-208-3

CONTENTS

Introduction iv

Common Module: Texts and Human Experiences 1

What Does NESA Require for the Common Module? 3

Understanding the Common Module.......................................5

Why Study Poetry?...29

The Poet..36

Out of Time 39

Wild Grapes...47

Gulliver 54

Vesper-Song of the Reverend Samuel Marsden..........................60

William Street...67

Beach Burial 73

Ideas 83

The Essay...90

Annotated Related Material 94

Other Related Texts 113

TOP NOTES SERIES

This series has been created to assist HSC students of English in their understanding of set texts. Top Notes are easy to read, providing analysis of issues and discussion of important ideas contained in the texts.

Particular care has been taken to ensure that students are able to examine each text in the context of the module it has been allocated to.

Each text generally includes:

- Notes on the specific module
- Plot summary
- Character analysis
- Setting
- Thematic concerns
- Language studies
- Essay questions and a modelled response
- Other textual material
- Study practice questions
- Useful quotes

We have covered the areas we feel are important for students in their study of *Texts and Human Experiences* for their Common Module. I am sure you will find these Top Notes useful in your studies of English.

Bruce Pattinson
Series Editor

COMMON MODULE:
TEXTS AND HUMAN EXPERIENCES

"It is quite possible—overwhelmingly probable, one might guess—that we will always learn more about human life and personality from novels than from scientific psychology"

NOAM CHOMSKY

What is the Common Module?

The Common Module set for the 2019–23 HSC is *Texts and Human Experiences*. It is compulsory to study this topic as prescribed by NESA and it is common to all three English courses. Remember: you will be learning how texts reveal individual and collective human experiences. There are no right or wrong answers in this module – it is about how you see and interpret material and engage with it.

In the Common Module you will be analysing one prescribed text and a range of short texts that are related to the idea of human experiences. You will analyse texts not only to investigate the ideas they present about this area but also how they convey these ideas. This means you will be looking closely at the techniques a composer uses to represent his / her messages and shape meaning. You will also be looking at relationships between texts in regard to the experiences you explore. Overall, you will become an expert on texts and the human experience — that is, the different notions people have about human experience and the various ways composers manipulate techniques to communicate their ideas about it.

Specifically you will look at one set text from the following list.

- Doerr, Anthony, *All the Light We Cannot See*
- Lohrey, Amanda, *Vertigo*
- Orwell, George, *Nineteen Eighty-Four*
- Parrett, Favel, *Past the Shallows*
- Dobson, Rosemary 'Young Girl at a Window', 'Over the Hill', 'Summer's End', 'The Conversation', 'Cock Crow', 'Amy Caroline', 'Canberra Morning'
- Slessor, Kenneth 'Wild Grapes', 'Gulliver', 'Out of Time', 'Vesper-Song of the Reverend Samuel Marsden', 'William Street', 'Beach Burial'
- Harrison, Jane, *Rainbow's End*
- Miller, Arthur, *The Crucible*
- Shakespeare, William, *The Merchant of Venice*
- Winton, Tim, *The Boy Behind the Curtain* Chapters: 'Havoc: A Life in Accidents', 'Betsy', 'Twice on Sundays', 'The Wait and the Flow', 'In the Shadow of the Hospital', 'The Demon Shark', 'Barefoot in the Temple of Art'
- Yousafzai, Malala & Lamb, Christina, *I am Malala*
- Daldry, Stephen, *Billy Elliot*
- O'Mahoney, Ivan, *Go Back to Where You Came From* – Series 1, Episodes 1, 2 and 3 and *The Response*
- Walker, Lucy, *Waste Land*

NESA has mandated that students must study a related text as part of the common module, and that this should be part of their in-school assessment. However there is NO LONGER a requirement to write about a related text in the HSC examination itself.

WHAT DOES NESA REQUIRE FOR THE COMMON MODULE?

The NESA documentation of the Common Module: Texts and Human Experiences states that students:

- deepen their understanding of how texts represent individual and collective human experiences;
- examine how texts represent human qualities and emotions associated with, or arising from, these experiences;
- appreciate, explore, interpret, analyse and evaluate the ways language is used to shape these representations in a range of texts in a variety of forms, modes and media;
- explore how texts may give insight into the anomalies, paradoxes and inconsistencies in human behaviour and motivations, inviting the responder to see the world differently, to challenge assumptions, ignite new ideas or reflect personally;
- may also consider the role of storytelling throughout time to express and reflect particular lives and cultures;
- by responding to a range of texts, further develop skills and confidence using various literary devices, language concepts, modes and media to formulate a considered response to texts;
- study one prescribed text and a range of short texts that provide rich opportunities to further explore representations of human experiences illuminated in texts;

- make increasingly informed judgements about how aspects of these texts, for example, context, purpose, structure, stylistic and grammatical features, and form shape meaning;
- select one related text and draw from personal experience to make connections between themselves, the world of the text and their wider world;
- by responding and composing throughout the module, further develop a repertoire of skills in comprehending, interpreting and analysing complex texts;
- examine how different modes and media use visual, verbal and/or digital language elements;
- communicate ideas using figurative language to express universal themes and evaluative language to make informed judgements about texts;
- further develop skills in using metalanguage, correct grammar and syntax to analyse language and express a personal perspective about a text

If this is what is required by NESA, we need to examine the concept of human experience carefully so we can adequately respond in these ways. I would recommend that you read the complete document which is on the NESA web site and can be downloaded in Word or Adobe. Understanding this document is an important step in handling the textual material within the guidelines required—remember you are reading for a purpose and should make notes and highlight ideas as you read so that you can develop these ideas later.

UNDERSTANDING THE COMMON MODULE

What are Human Experiences?

The concept of Human Experiences is at the heart of the Common Module.

Human Experiences are experiences of individuals or a group of people (eg a family, society, or nation) in life. There are a very wide range of human experiences which include but go beyond this list:

- feelings or reactions (momentary or long term): love, hate, anger, joy, fear, disgust
- key milestones or stages: birth, childhood, adulthood, marriage, divorce, death
- culture, belonging and identity
- conformity and rebellion
- innocence and guilt, justice
- freedom and repression
- education, vocation, work, sport, leisure
- attraction to a person, idea, group or cause
- opposition to an idea, cause, political system
- religious faith or belief
- extreme events such as an earthquake, avalanche, tsuanami
- regular events such as walking, eating, singing, dancing, discussing ideas.

The word *experience* seems innately connected to the human condition and it is something we have each day whether a mundane experience that is repetitive, or something new and dramatic which offers challenges and rewards. Experiences can vary greatly in their impact on individuals, groups and countries. One example might be a war that is a negative experience for a whole population while we may experience the wonder of medicine with a new vaccine for a deadly disease that saves millions of people. We need to note that the module asks for 'experiences' ...we are a combination of different experiences and each has a varying impact. One person's problem is another's challenge depending on perspective, skill set, previous experience and ability.

Experiences are widespread and often shared: this is why people tell their stories and these shared experiences form part of our cultural heritage. These experiences often inform, warn and teach across entire cultural groups and many stories are shared across cultures.

DEFINING HUMAN EXPERIENCES

Now let's attempt to define what human experiences are and shape them into a more coherent and easily understood framework so we can begin our investigation at a basic level of understanding before moving into more complex analysis and looking at how the texts illuminate our understanding of the term.

Dictionary.com defines the term **experience** as:

noun

1. a particular instance of personally encountering or undergoing something:
2. the process or fact of personally observing, encountering, or undergoing something:
3. the observing, encountering, or undergoing of things generally as they occur in the course of time:
   to learn from experience; the range of human experience.
4. knowledge or practical wisdom gained from what one has observed, encountered, or undergone, e.g. *a man of experience.*
5. *Philosophy.* the totality of the cognitions given by perception; all that is perceived, understood, and remembered.

verb

(used with object), **experienced, experiencing.**

6. to have experience of; meet with; undergo; feel, e.g. *to experience nausea.*
7. to learn by experience.

idiom

8. **experience religion**, to undergo a spiritual conversion by which one gains or regains faith in God.

Obviously there are a number of definitions according to context, but all are applicable to our study in some shape or form, as the range of human experience is so vast. The search for 'new experience' has driven much of the development of people, groups, cultures and nations over past millennia. New experiences are always met with excitement and often trepidation as to what change they might bring.

Think historically about how people have reacted to change. It can cause great upheavals in society, with violent reactions while other changes brought through various experiences are welcomed and may change how people live and comprehend the world. Experiences affect us emotionally in many cases rather than logically and when we respond emotionally, behaviours become unpredictable. This causes the paradoxes, anomalies and inconsistencies mentioned in the rubric. If we were logical beings the world would be an easier place, but probably more boring.

These definitions all point to the fact that memory is the key to experience. The experience is stored in memory and drawn upon when the circumstances are repeated or closely mimicked so we can deal with them — hopefully better than on the initial experience.

Experiences can come in many ways and the synonyms listed below for experience help us to understand the concept even further. They assist in defining how an experience can arise:

Synonyms

actions	understanding	judgment
background	wisdom	observation
contacts	acquaintances	perspicacity
involvement	actuality	practicality
know-how	caution	proofs
maturity	combat	savoir-faire
participation	doings	seasonings
patience	empiricism	sophistication
practice	evidence	strife
reality	existences	trials
sense	exposures	worldliness
skill	familiarity	forebearance
struggle	intimacy	
training	inwardness	

http://www.thesaurus.com/browse/experience?s=t

These synonyms show partly the vast array of words that our language has created around this concept, and also shows how important it is in the human psyche. We, as humans, want to experience. Now we will look at some examples of experiences and examine how they can have an impact. It is also important to remember that experiences do not have to be positive. You might experience a huge problem, a bereavement, a car accident, an unwelcome relationship or something totally bizarre that rocks your world. There can be a more opaque side to any experience that may need to be addressed.

The whole aim of this Common Module is to examine the text closely but also relate it to the concept of human experiences and decide how examining it in this way enables us to better understand both the text and the concept of humanity.

It is important that you unpack what each text you study shows you about human experiences and what ideas / themes arise from those experiences. Formulate your own ideas about the text.

Read the NESA Stage 6 document called *English Stage 6: Annotations of selected texts prescribed for the Higher School Certificate 2019–23* (see *www.educationstandards.nsw.edu.au*) for the set text you are studying. This document offers insights into the way each particular text should be examined by outlining key ideas and areas for clarification.

Human experiences and ways of experiencing vary due to individual circumstance and these experiences can change many things about individual lives, communities and the world. When we examine the concept of human experience in relation to a text, we need to examine the assumptions or biases we bring to it as well as how experiencing the text itself may change us and how we view things. The text may challenge and confront how we view the human experience or we may have preconceived ideas that make it more difficult for this to happen.

Students can also think about their own 'personal experience to make connections between themselves, the world of the text and their wider world.' Examining and enjoying any text is an experience in itself but it is what we take away from the text and apply that is the crucial aspect. That is not to say that every text will be enjoyed or offer a human experience that is significant either positively or negatively. Some texts may not personally engage you and that is fine. This is especially so when you begin to look for other related material that links to *Texts and Human Experiences*. We recommend that you find examples of texts that link but also personally appeal to you so that you can relate empathetically with them.

Individual Human Experiences

The idea of personal experiences is a popular and pervasive concept, especially in the literature of many cultures. Recording personal experiences as a means of sharing wisdom or more mundane daily tasks is part of human nature and we record and relate these experiences frequently. Experiences are recorded and relayed in many ways. We tell oral stories in both anecdotal and formal ways, we write, draw, sing and photograph our way into history (or not). Look at the proliferation of social media in this current century as people record their daily, even hourly, experiences for all to see. We record the most trivial details of our lives for likes and followers while the real world passes us by. Human experiences affect us on a daily basis and some experiences influence our lives and the way we live them.

Individuals seek out experiences in a variety of ways. Some seek more and more extreme experiences to test themselves against the world. Others limit their experiences. A lot of people prefer the familiar and don't actively seek new experiences. Individuals, it must be remembered, also see experiences in different ways and the same experience may have a very different impact on individuals. The one thing we can be certain about is that experiences are part of humanity and even the most limited of us have them. Many of these experiences also come from interaction with others and as noted we also like to share these experiences.

Experiences are what define us in many ways and are what makes us human.

We are going to look at four specific ways that experiences can influence us as people over the next few pages. These are physical, psychological, emotional and intellectual experiences and many experiences are a combination of these.

Physical Experience

The concept of a physical experience is tied into the human experience and part of the collective experience as well. Individuals seek physical experiences to test themselves against nature and other individuals often as part of trials and rituals, for example being integrated into a community. In modern times individuals have sought to test themselves with extreme sports and explorations into the harshest conditions and even space. Physical experiences can also change the way we see the world and others because of the chemical changes these experiences have on our bodies and mind. Physical experiences are often challenges and part of the experience is overcoming adversity. These physical challenges are often celebrated, as in the case of sports, but can also offer challenges if the experience is a negative one such as an accident or disease. Physical experiences are also often quite public and thus have permeated our societies in both their execution and how they are perceived. These physical experiences, even if experienced vicariously, have become popular across cultures and celebrated. Think of examples for yourself but most competitive sports offer examples.

Bruce Lee extends the concept of the physical experience into all aspects of life and that's what we will look at next in our analysis of human experiences –

'If you always put limits on everything you do, physical or anything else, it will spread into your work and into your life. There are no limits. There are only plateaus, and you must not stay there, you must go beyond them.'

Psychological Experience

The idea of a psychological experience is tied into many of the abstract ideas that people experience and can lead to a discussion of what is normal psychology. From the earliest times humans have attempted to alter their psychology through a number of experiences. On a simple level this can be a drug that changes the person's or group's perspective on reality. Examples of this might be alcohol or marijuana but cultural groups also use various substances to share group experiences. This can be seen in Native American cultures with *peyote*. In more modern times prescription drugs that are mood altering have been used to minimise the symptoms of psychiatric illnesses such as depression, and these mood altering drugs are common and legal. Others attempt to alter their psychology by seeing specialists in this area while others act out their condition leading to social and criminal issues. When discussing the human experience, psychology is a key issue and will form a part of most studies of experience. When taken too far this search for a new psychological experience can be harmful eg. an addiction.

Carl Jung, the famous psychologist, comments on the problems of addiction for human experiences, stating clearly that excess can be an issue:

"Every form of addiction is bad, no matter whether the narcotic be alcohol, morphine or idealism."

Emotional Experience

According to the psychologist, Robert Plutchik, there are eight basic emotions:

- **Fear** — feeling afraid.
- **Anger** — feeling angry. A stronger word for anger is rage.
- **Sadness** — feeling sad. Other words are sorrow, grief (a stronger feeling, for example when someone has died) or **depression** (feeling sad for a long time without any external cause). Some people think depression is a different emotion.
- **Joy** — feeling happy. Other words are happiness, gladness.
- **Disgust** — feeling something is wrong or nasty
- **Trust** — a positive emotion; admiration is stronger; **acceptance** is weaker
- **Anticipation** — in the sense of looking forward positively to something which is going to happen. **Expectation** is more neutral; **dread** is more negative.

https://simple.wikipedia.org/wiki/List_of_emotions

Emotions are the strongest drivers of human experience and form lasting aspects of any experience. Think about breaking up with someone you love and the emotions that drive behaviours in this situation. People have all sorts of extreme behaviours under the influence of emotions and these experiences are often the ones recorded and those which influence us most. Think about the role emotions play in our lives and the range of emotions from the list above. Consider how much emotions affect our life experiences, how they influence our decisions which decide our experiences and on a higher level consider how they affect the decisions which may seriously impact our experiences, such as politicians going to war.

Intellectual Experience

The concept of an intellectual experience is linked to decisions and experiences we have based on analysis and logic rather than the emotional choices referred to in the previous section. These intellectual experiences have changed the way we live and how we have seen our world. These experiences have affected the way we as humans have altered our world to suit our needs and lead to all the great advances in human society and thus experiences. Changes in our ideas, beliefs etc. alter the way we interact with the world and often these intellectual changes come at great cost.

Think of the time in Europe when the Church dominated and stopped scientific advances by calling them heresy/witchcraft. Open societies are more open to new ideas and this is what has hastened the pace of intellectual experiences as dominant ideologies fall away. Intellectual advances may not have the excitement that the other types produce but perhaps they have a more lasting impact on people, societies and the world in general. Ideas are powerful experiences and people hold beliefs strongly.

Immanuel Kant stated that:

> *"experience without theory is blind, but theory without experience is mere intellectual play."*

Consider this statement in the light of what we have learnt about human experiences. Are they a combination of many factors or can we isolate experiences into simple forms?

What exactly is a human experience?

The titular question reminds us of the old brainteaser: "If a tree falls in a forest and no one is around to hear it, does it make a sound?"

There are two classic responses to this. The more Platonically-minded would say the tree always makes a sound when it falls in the forest. We don't have to be there to hear it; we can imagine the sound of a tree falling in the forest, based on memory of such an event or on the recording of such an event. We know that sound is just vibrating air, and it's safe to say that air always vibrates in response to a tree falling, or a bear growling, or a cicada singing, whether we are there to hear it or not.

The second answer is a more post-structuralist response: the sound doesn't occur on its own; it needs a human ear to be heard. Therefore, if there is no human in the forest to hear the tree fall, then there is no sound. This automatically implies that "experience" of anything requires the presence of a human being, which means there is no such thing as an experience that *isn't* human.

Animal rights activists – or anyone with a beloved pet – would almost certainly reject this notion because it prioritises humans and relegates all other species to a lower class of being: an attitude that most would agree has gotten the human race into an awful lot of environmental trouble over the last 200 years of industrialisation.

In his article (*What is an Experience?*), my learned colleague Paul Hartley describes experience in its most basic form, as "the perception of something else" and "ultimately information about what we have perceived." But does this make it particularly human? Dogs and cats perceive things. Insects perceive things. You could even say that plants perceive things, such as the direction from which the sun is shining. Perception is the most basic of life's survival tools for all manner of flora and fauna.

In her brief but cogent disquisition on the subject (*What is Human?*), another of my learned colleagues, Nadine Hare, asserts that to be human is a social construct. Hartley builds on that notion by suggesting that culture affects experience when we start to share it, because "the words, associations, and priorities we attach to the shared experience define how we understand the world we live in."

Hare rightly points out that this world is increasingly dominated by consumerism, which has distorted what it means to be human by excluding all of the attributes and qualities that "make people people." Calling us consumers reduces our experiences to mere transactions. It defines human experience within the narrow confines of the purchase funnel and has little interest in anything that isn't a purchase driver.

Perhaps the field of commerce is where the experiential rubber most emphatically meets the road. Unlike mere perception, commerce is a uniquely human experience. It has mediated, automated, and dominated the human agenda to the point where we are defined by what we buy and little else. Commerce has invaded the non-profit spheres of government, health, and education, imposing its own priorities and principles on these institutions in the expectation that they will behave more like businesses. And even though business still strives to appeal to the so-called masses, it prioritises the pursuit of individual wealth, and in so doing, not only inhibits the desire for shared experience but unravels the social fabric historically woven by the democratic tradition.

As if in response, that social fabric is being re-woven by our networks. As Hare asserts, "humans both produce technology and are produced through technology." Experience is shared more now than it ever has been because the experiential platform – i.e., that very human invention called the internet – is in place to facilitate it like never before, and on a global scale.

This sharing capability reintroduces all of those things that "make people people" back into the conversation – whether commercial or political. What "makes people people" is messy, unpredictable, emotional, and complex. Most of what makes us human has no place in the experiential confines of the purchase funnel, and defies any of our attempts to place it there.

The challenge for us as a species is to embrace this new capacity for sharing to keep the agendas of our hegemonic institutions – whether commercial or political – from defining what makes an experience human. A post-consumer business strategy might be one that, as Hare hopes, will "expand our view of people to include the complex and dynamic social, cultural, gendered, spiritual and racialised beings that they are." Maybe then will our shared human experience truly become, as Hartley asserts, the glue that holds us all together as human beings.

Will Novosedlik
MISC magazine

https://miscmagazine.com/what-is-a-human-experience/

This article appeared in the September 2014 edition of MISC magazine. Can you relate to what the article says about human experiences? Do human experiences depend on perception? Does the experience of anything require the presence of a human as experiencer (para 3)? Can the ideas of experience be extended to include perception by plants or animals? Hartley's idea is that "shared human experience" is "the glue that holds us all together as human beings". Is this an oversimplification?

The Impact of Human Experiences

Human experiences have impacts on many levels. On an individual level, we can have changes in our assumptions about the world and people around us; we can ingest new ideas and have these open new vistas of productivity and performance. We can also reflect and build on these experiences to ensure that they are even more meaningful to our lives. Behaviours towards others and the way we respond to the world can manifest themselves in new and different responses. An example might be that through adverse experiences we can build resilience so that the next negative experience isn't as traumatic and we accept it for what it is. Experiences also teach us new behaviours on a very physical level—if you burn yourself once on a flame you learn not to do it again (hopefully).

The impact of human experiences can also be shared in groups and societies. Firstly, let's examine some group dynamics that can be affected by human experiences. Groups share experiences and adapt and develop behaviours that impact on the group as a whole. Think about the notorious 'bonding' sessions sporting teams have that unite them in a common goal. Think about the behaviours of various gangs in our society. We see plenty of examples of this on American television where gangs based on ethnicity and social groupings form specific sets of behaviours that impact on how they interact with each other and the world. These groupings carry assumptions about how they see the world and respond to it. For example, they may have generally negative reactions to law enforcement and this is ingrained into their codes of behaviour. They are suspicious of the world and the people in it—dividing them up into threats, the law and victims. These behaviours are often reinforced by group experiences such as the initiation rituals which are integral to membership.

Often the impact of these behaviours is to perpetuate stereotypes that then categorise the individuals within these groups. The graphic I have included here shows a stereotypical gang member with the suspicious gaze, ubiquitous hoody and scruffy look. These stereotypes reject new ideas and maintain assumptions about the world, often to the detriment of their members. The experiences they have reinforce their own stereotypical way of viewing anything outside the safety of the group and the cycle continues. Of course, other groups have more positive impacts and see the world as a very different place and their experiences are designed to be positive interactions. Think about groups such as Rotary who are constructive in the community. Other groups have specialty interests such as Animal Welfare, Surf Lifesaving and charities.

Normal social interactions impact groups and individuals, but it takes a major event to alter the behaviours of whole societies, especially so in the modern world where societies are large in scale. Earlier in human history smaller experiences could alter the behaviour of societies as they were insignificant in size compared to modern ones. We often fail to remember that many of these ancient societies' behaviours were impacted by superstition, religions and cultural habituation. The modern society as we know it is only a recent phenomenon. Just a few hundred years ago with church rule people were forced to think in a specific

way and punished for not adhering to a theological culture. Think of the Spanish Inquisition, the imprisonment of Galileo and other such restrictions on freedom of thought; scientific breakthroughs were hidden or declared witchcraft. Even recently the world has seen societies kept repressed by failed ideologies. The brutality of such regimes has left deep scars on the social psyche of nations as they try to recover. This has had an impact on the human experiences of whole populations, and societies respond accordingly.

One example might be at the conclusion of the Communist regime in East Germany when the Berlin Wall was destroyed as a visual symbol of the new-found freedom of a whole population of people who had been repressed for decades by a brutal and ever-present regime. Many citizens who had grown up in this system, where you could 'disappear' without trial or real evidence, found the idea that you could express yourself incredible. Many of the

East Germans couldn't believe that this freedom was real and that the Stasi (the secret police) were gone.

Other experiences can affect societies in extreme ways. Think about wars and the impact they have on civilian populations.

Climatic events such as earthquakes change the way that people behave and respond to situations. Catastrophic flooding occurred in the US city of New Orleans in 2005. The US President's response to help was not immediate and the national administration was severely criticised for lack of effective action.

Societies also respond to perceived problems such as pollution. In 1989 the oil tanker Exxon Valdez ran aground in Prince William Sound, Alaska with disastrous results. The effects of this event are still being experienced thirty years later.

Societies can be divided, as we saw with the election of Donald Trump in the United States of America and the reaction of the Political Left.

The impact of human experiences on societies can be quite dramatic, as we have seen, while other experiences (such as an election) can go by without a murmur from societies, no matter who wins. As a last thought before we move on you should also consider the impact of the media on societies in the modern world, and how they influence individuals, societies and the development of ideas.

Problems With Human Behaviour

So far, we have discussed the impact of human experiences on behaviour. Now we can begin to develop some more complex judgements and understandings about the impact of those experiences on human behaviours. In simplistic terms it could be assessed as:

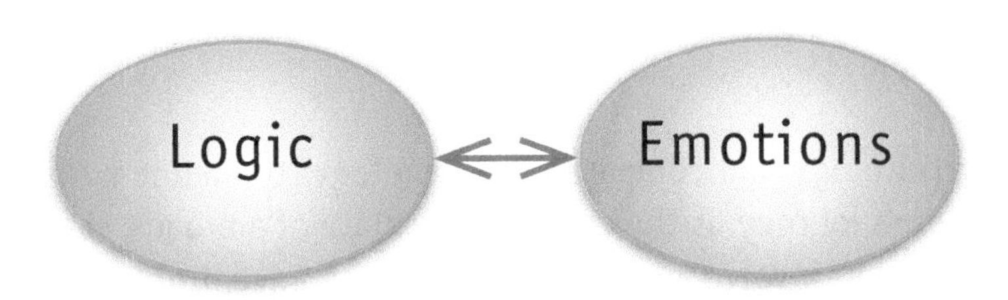

These two opposites on the continuum certainly shape the manner in which we see incidents and how they affect the experience. For instance, if someone you love has no interest in you, it creates a very different reaction to someone you don't care about having no interest in you. It is generally agreed that humans respond more strongly with emotion than they do with logic. Often, it is only through time and reflection that we can understand how an experience has changed and/or altered the manner in which we see a situation or individual.

The Role of Storytelling in Human Experiences

Storytelling has been part of the human experience since 'people' began communicating and it is a method used to convey information and experience as well as be entertaining. Earliest myths were all oral and then people began to write down stories so they weren't lost in time. From this, various theories have developed around storytelling and one is the 'monomyth', which is a template across cultures for storytelling. Let's have a look at this below.

'In narratology and comparative mythology, the monomyth, or the hero's journey, is the common template of a broad category of tales that involve a hero who goes on an adventure, and in a decisive crisis wins a victory, and then comes home changed or transformed.

The concept was introduced in *The Hero with a Thousand Faces* (1949) by Joseph Campbell, who described the basic narrative pattern as follows:

> "A hero ventures forth from the world of common day into a region of supernatural wonder: fabulous forces are there encountered and a decisive victory is won: the hero comes back from this mysterious adventure with the power to bestow boons on his fellow man."

Campbell and other scholars, such as Erich Neumann, describe narratives of Gautama Buddha, Moses, and Christ in terms of the monomyth. Critics argue that the concept is too broad or general to be of much use in comparative mythology. Others say that the hero's journey is only a part of the monomyth; the other part is a sort of different form, or colour, of the hero's journey.

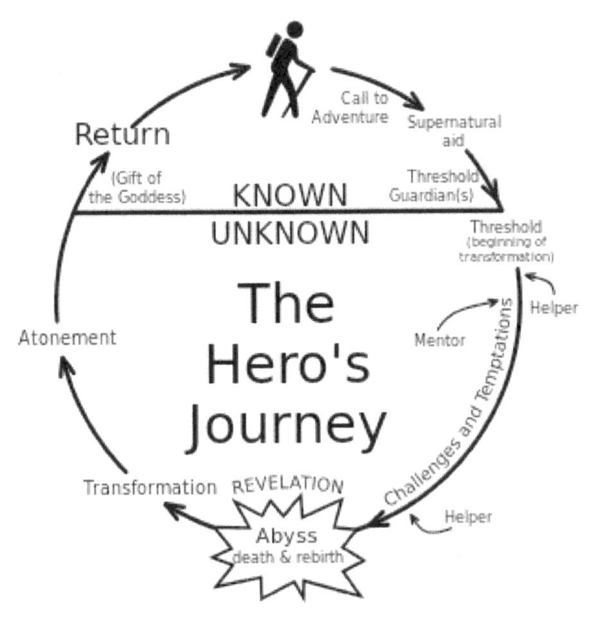

https://en.wikipedia.org/wiki/Hero%27s_journey

Storytelling in History and its Purpose in Human Experience

Storytelling in oral form was accompanied by some theatrics to make the stories as entertaining as possible. Many of the early narratives were based upon religious ceremonies and stories of the creation of the earth and people(s). As time moved on, these stories were accompanied by dance, music and/or theatre and often were part of lengthy rituals, often taking days. These stories were designed to bring meaning to people's lives by explaining their own existence and the purpose/meaning of life in a time when life expectancy was short and entertainment was scarce. Of course stories were also recorded as these experiences were significant to all people and these stories run across all cultures. Before writing, stories were recorded in pictures such as cave art, in tattoo designs on skin and in designs such as rock piles and the giant carved heads of Easter Island.

Writing changed the manner in which stories were told and many of the old oral traditions were lost, barely being kept alive by specialists. Stories began to travel across cultural and national boundaries on whatever surface could be created. Papyrus, bones, pottery, skins, paper and in more modern times film, video and digital storage have changed, over time, the way in which stories of human experience have been told and shared. Content evolved from myth, fable and legend to history, personal narratives and commentary. Modern narrative form often has an educational or didactic element and can drift into propaganda. Stories of self-revelation can be instructive and give audiences the opportunity to apply learning to individual lives, whereas historically narrative was used in this way for societies and groups as a whole. In recent times narratives have become interactive and audiences can choose how the narrative unfolds.

Whatever form the story takes we all have a seemingly innate need for narratives to make sense of our lives. They either confirm our world view or alter our world view depending on the experience they convey and the experiences that we bring to the narrative. We need to remember that narratives are important to human experience and have been significant since the beginning of time.

The Text as an Experience

The concept of the text as an experience is one area to consider as we look at *Texts and Human Experiences*. Reading or viewing the text is an experience in itself and when we do this we bring our own history (experiences) to the text and this helps shape our understanding.

Think about the personal perspective that you bring to a text. What are some of your experiences that might influence how you read a particular text? Some texts, especially personal narratives of trial and tribulation or loss, can be confronting to some audiences and bring back strong opinions or emotions. Many texts attempt to do this as they convey a particular point of view about the world.

Does what you bring to the text affect what you learn from that text? We also need to delve into how the narrative experience is conveyed and how this in turn impacts upon the manner in which the story is received by audiences across different cultures. For example, Western films where heroes fight Islamic terrorism may well be viewed very differently by audiences in Western democracies and Islamic countries. Even seemingly innocuous narratives like the movie 'The Red Pill' which is about men's rights and created by a woman, has caused a polarisation of views wherever it has been shown. Strong personal experiences and viewpoints certainly bring their own understandings to texts.

Questions for Texts and Human Experiences

- Define the module in your own words.
- How are people connected by shared experiences?
- How might physical experience(s) change the way you respond to the world?
- How do you think a person's context and prior experiences shape how they perceive the world?
- Are experiences unique or do prior experiences have an impact on a current experience and way of seeing life?
- What is positive about human experiences?
- Discuss what is negative about human experiences.
- To what extent does experience shape the way we see other people and / or groups?
- Is an individual's culture part of their experience or is it something else?
- Is it possible not to have any meaningful experiences at all?
- Why do people tell stories?
- What do you think you might learn from a narrative?

WHY STUDY POETRY?

Poetry is a part of life and is about life. It deals with all the emotions of life: love, death, nature, friendship, feelings of pain, anger, frustration – all the moods and ideas that are part of the human condition. Poetry appeals to our understanding through our imagination, making us see what the poet has seen, hear what the poet has heard and experience his feelings. This is particularly true of Slessor with his use of the senses and time to convey human experiences in a meaningful manner.

Useful Literary Terms

Familiarity with the following terms of figurative language, poetic device and technique will enable you to convince your examiner that you have acquired the vocabulary necessary to discuss how the composer attempts to share his ideas through the use of his poetic craft. Remember this is an outcome of your course!

Alliteration repetition of initial consonant sounds close together – for a special/poetic sound effect/ emphasis (e.g. "one summer's evening soaked").

Allusion a reference to something from history, literature, religion that adds to its meaning

Analysis to examine closely, take apart for the purpose of greater understanding.

Assonance repetition of vowel sounds in words or lines close together.

Cliché	word or phrase which is very common and overused.
Climax	where emotions/ideas reach their a peak (often the end of a poem).
Criticism	evaluation of literature, finding strong points which support the meaning, looking at style and language use.
Dissonance	harsh sounding words together for a special effect and emphasis.
Enjambment	run-on-lines, with no punctuation pauses, having effect on the sense of the lines in the poem
Free verse	a disregard for traditional rhyme/rhythm rules
Hyperbole	exaggeration for effect/emphasis (e.g. 'millionth person').
Imagery	figures of speech – metaphors, similes etc. that make word pictures, comparisons or contrasts, to aid understanding
Irony	a reversal of expected ideas used to make an effect, to draw attention to a point.
Juxtaposition	two contrasting ideas close together for dramatic effect and emphasis
Lyric	a poem that expresses emotions and ideas.
Metaphor	a direct comparison between two things, referring to one in terms of another – without using 'like' or 'as'

Mood	overall emotional effect/feeling set in a line or stanza of a poem.
Motif	dominant theme/object that comes up several times in a poem or collection of poems
Narrative	style of writing which relates a story
Onomatopoeia	words that imitate sound being described, used for the sound effect and emphasis (e.g. "whirred with an insect nervousness").
Paradox	a contradiction which actually is true
Personification	to give human qualities to non-living things (e.g. "all the sun's disciples cloaked")
Realism	make vividly real by careful attention to detail
Satire	criticise by means of subtle ridicule, with comic effect
Simile	comparison used to describe something more vividly, using 'like' or 'as', to get a certain meaning across
Stanza	divisions within a poem, similar to paragraphs in prose.
Structure	the shape or form of a poem, the way it hangs together
Style	interplay of structure/ language/ tone that supports the theme
Symbol	an image that stands for a complex idea
Theme	central message/meaning of a piece of writing (e.g. memory)

Tone overall attitude conveyed by the writing to the audience through the combination of subject, mood and style

Transferred epithet figurative language where an idea is passed from one thing onto another for dramatic immediacy

THEME / IDEA

Theme or idea is an important aspect of any literature. Try always to find the idea in a poem, in other words, the *central thread that runs through it* that gives it its unique meaning. Often the title of the poem is the key to its meaning, so look there first. The title of a poem, or story or film is not decided on a whim – the composer puts a great deal of thought into it, and thus to appreciate the text one should give good thought to the title, and any sub-title.

Remember that the poet is presenting his ideas, feelings and arguments about life as he sees it. The reader has to work these out, and different readers may come up with different interpretations, and we may never know for certain exactly what the poet's meaning is. Reading poetry can become very subjective (personal) as the reader recognises feelings and sympathises with the ideas, but poetry analysis must show the interpretation is underpinned at all times by the text itself.

STYLE

Poetry is a particular and special literary art form, and it is the style of writing that makes it different from the prose of novels. The reader should pay attention to the method of writing because a good poet will be very deliberate about this. There are many formal poetic devices that have been used down the ages to express a poet's ideas and emotions

(rhyme, rhythm, language, punctuation etc). Modern poetry is not as disciplined as, for instance, a sonnet by Shakespeare which was limited to 14 lines and a distinct rhyme scheme.

However, that does not mean that there is no 'style' to the poetry. It just may not be obvious at first – but it needs to be found through close scrutiny.

Refer to the literary terms above and see what has been used and how the poet has used it to convey his theme, look at the stanza divisions, note the punctuation, pick up the sound effects of alliteration and assonance. Remember that the manner in which the poet does his work is as important as the meaning.

Outlined here are some of Slessor's stylistic features. Find your own examples from the poems for each and note them in the space provided.

1. Slessor was inspired by the harbour and so uses water imagery in many of his poems.

   ____

   ____

   ____

   ____

2. Tight form – Slessor often uses very regular rhyme scheme, rhythm patterns and cyclic structure

   ____

   ____

   ____

3. Frequent use of poetic devices such as alliteration, assonance and onomatopoeia add aural resonance. He often recreates a scene aurally just as effectively as visually.

____

____

____

4. Sensual imagery is used to represent experiences vividly, making them appeal to our senses

____

____

____

5. Metaphor is used to enhance mood and atmosphere as well as to represent the complex themes relating to time, life and death.

____

____

____

6. The connotations of specific words and phrase choices in the various poems allow Slessor to introduce layers of meaning into the experiences he represents.

____

____

____

THE POET

Kenneth Slessor was born at Orange, New South Wales on the 27th March 1901. He was educated in Sydney and on leaving school became a reporter. His life's work was writing and he was the leader writer and book reviewer on the Sydney *Daily Telegraph* in the years before his death. One other job that was important to his poetry was that he was a war correspondent with the Australian Army from 1940-44. It was during this period that he wrote 'Beach Burial'.

His work *One Hundred Poems* contains all the poems that Slessor considered worth presenting. Preceding his death in 1971 he was not prolific in writing poetry and seems to have completed his major works much earlier. Many see his greatest work as 'Five Bells'. Slessor's career is important as it gives his poetry a sense of place and feeling.

Slessor spent most of his life in Sydney, and its harbour, streets and buildings are the basis and background for some of the poems set for study. He captures in his descriptions a true sense of the magnificence and excitement of Sydney. Buckley said of Slessor's work, "His best poems are nearly all concerned with simple situations or with people". The reader can appreciate this when reading 'Wild Grapes', 'Gulliver' or 'Beach Burial'.

Slessor's work falls roughly into three periods, the first of which is concerned with history, romance, fantasy and legend. The second period of work begins the transition to the more modernist techniques and approaches from his romantic fantasies. This period shows Slessor developing his concept of the sea and more concrete images that the reader can identify with more readily. It is here, as Moore says, “He surprises with wholly original images and delights with the sharp pungency of pictorial words”. It is this pictorial language and concrete, yet sensuous, imagery that begin to mark Slessor’s work.

The third period of his work is undoubtedly that which gave him his reputation as a poet. The poems of this period present pictures that appeal to the senses and develop his themes to their fullest depth with contemporary and vivid images. Yet these poems still have a feel of time passing and impermanence, a constant theme in all his work. Fitzgerald suggests this theme is an expression of his frustration with reaching an understanding of time and its intricacies. This frustration is expressed as an image of glass. For example in ‘Five Bells’ Joe’s ghost presses his face “in agonies of speech on speechless panes”. The glass withholds something and that is Slessor’s frustration. Many see this as indicating his work is overwhelmingly pessimistic but others firmly believe his poetry never becomes totally disillusioned.

In fact his thematic concerns also include the struggle for the meaning of life and how a profound love of beauty brings joy to the poet. In exploring these themes he examines humanity with the universal themes of life, death and change but in a quintessentially Australian way. He manages this by writing about images that are concrete and visible. Images that a reader can respond to such as sleep, the harbour and the environment.

Slessor’s poetic persona, and probably the man himself, is always struggling to avoid the significant limitation of time yet he captures moments in time much like a photographer. This accounts for the frustration in the poetry mentioned before. Slessor accepts in his poetry the passing of time brings change and he records this passing with distinct references in the poems. For example in 'Country Towns' (not a prescribed poem but a clear example) there is "1860 over their doors" and "dated a year and a half ago". These references place each object clearly in time and shows the power time has over all things.

The feelings of nostalgia and memory that are interwoven into the poetry show that it is not all pessimism in his poetry. He also looks at the issue of friendship and in particular the Australian idea of mateship in a positive way even though it may result in loss. Another idea that is relevant to his work is war and its effects and this is dealt with specifically in 'Beach Burial'. The recurring and potent image of the sea seen in this poem can also be found in many of his other poems.

The themes and subject matter are not just what makes his poetry unique and distinguishable but his technique which is based around construction of common images. The poet makes them vivid and intriguing despite his general simplicity of word choice and poetic diction. This language will be examined in detail in the individual analysis section.

To close this introductory section let Slessor himself point out the conflict between optimism and pessimism in his work,

> I think poetry is written mostly for pleasure, by which I mean the pleasure of pain, horror, anguish and awe as well as the pleasure of beauty, music and the act of living

Kenneth Slessor died in 1971 and still continues to bring sensual delight and thoughtful introspection with his poetry.

OUT OF TIME

Summary

This poem explores two of Slessor's favourite ideas – time and death. It is comprised of three sonnets that are meticulously structured and linked through their imagery and focus on time. In the poem Slessor uses an extended metaphor of time as a wave and water imagery to comment on time's relentless progress. Time is a powerful force that sweeps all along toward aging and death. Both these ideas are central to the human experience, both individually and collectively.

Glossary

foxed	Stained or spotted a yellow/brown colour by age
quince	A tree that grows a hard, fragrant, yellow fruit used for jams. Quince is also the name of the fruit.
slat	Long thin strips in this context it is the sun
skulk	To move in a sneaky/ stealthy way and/or to keep something hidden
vilely	Offensive, foul and/or repulsive

quench	In this context quench means to put out or extinguish
entreats	To make a sincere request
implore	To beg urgently or ask for mercy
meniscus	A crescent shaped body such as a lens or the surface of water where it is caused by tension. It seems to be neither in nor out of the liquid.

ANALYSIS

A note on sonnets...

Slessor is renowned for his tightly organised poetry and his use of the sonnet in this poem demonstrates this well. A sonnet is a fourteen line poem with a tight structure. This version has a rhyme scheme of ABAB CDCD EFEF GG and every line has ten syllables.

PART I

The first sonnet introduces the topic of time immediately. The poem is in the first person so the audience is brought close to the experience. The persona presents a powerful representation of time. The image of hundred yachts is forceful and magnificent. The movement "behind the daylight" alludes to time's movement as unseen. He compares time's relentless, shoving quality to the knife-like quality of the yellow streaks of sun pushing into the harbour. Here the reference to "quince-bright" is not only to colour but also emphasises hardness and bitterness like the fruit of the quince. Quince is an older fruit, more popular in years gone by to make jam.

In stanza two time is a wave. This water imagery is very effective as it captures both the continual nature and the actual erosive effects of time. It directly affects the persona and he speaks of its actions as it "enfolds me in its bed" and "runs me through". Here the killing aspect of time is raised. He refers to himself as "Skulker" which implies his fear and likens himself to objects that waves flow over and around when he states, "Time flows, not you!" He realises he cannot go on forever.

The movement of time is highlighted through the repetition of adverbs that end in 'ly'. This recreates the action and energy of time and sounds like a heart beat. The alliteration of the forceful consonant "d" in "drills me, drives me" echoes the authority and harshness of time. The comment "Time takes me" accentuates the persona's passive position. Like weed in the sea, he is moved by time, even changed by it.

The final couplet addresses time directly, personifying it with the capital. Time must continue and the "lovely moment" must be left. The use of "must" is absolute and reflects the poet's concern with the reality of time as perpetual motion. The rhyme of the sonnet, but especially of this couplet, creates a motion that mirrors the movement described.

Part II

The first line directly links to the final action in the last line of the sonnet before. This maintains the motion and his urge to move is stressed by the adjective "Eager". Time's multi-faceted affect on life are seen through the use of successive contrasts; "quench and ripen" and "kiss and kill". The line "Tomorrow begs him, breathless for his lack" refers to those who cannot wait for another day, presumably in excitement. Yet "beauty dead" tells of the decaying effects of time. Many wish time to stop to prevent beauty fading.

Yet stanza two reminds us that time has no choice – "he must open doors, Or close them". Here Slessor manipulates a well-known image of opening and closing doors (receiving or losing an opportunity) extending it as a metaphor to represent life. This reminds us of the continuum of life – birth and death occur constantly. The "pale and faceless host" can equally remind us of the fear and worry for a birth or a death.

The remarkable regular singsong rhythm of the third stanza reinforces the persistent progress of time. The hyperbole, "a million years", underscores the infinite expanse of time and hints at human unimportance. We cannot ever hope to keep such appointment.

The persona then refers to himself directly saying, "I and the moment laugh". This implies the persona has a somewhat youthful, uncaring attitude towards time concern about time's effects at that stage. Yet the "Leaning against his golden undertow" refers to the unseen movement below the wave that it resisted, perhaps unconsciously, or perhaps the ambivalence was an act. Either way, there is an attempt not to be moved by time.

PART III

Again, Slessor echoes the final lines of the last section in his opening line thereby maintaining the motion. He speaks of seeing the birds rise and an image of resistance by gulls flying against the wind is evoked. There is the idea that these birds are in their own vacuum. The meniscus is neither in nor out of the water but it is an optical effect. The implication that this state is not natural is suggested by their movement "backwards". It is clear that the gulls are not beyond time's effects by them dying in the final couplet.

He then sees the scene protected from time. The solid shape of the beach, sand water and peninsula seem fixed but, of course, despite their solidness they are changing. This image is like a photograph, "Lensed in a bubble's ghostly camera" and only "The moment's world". It is an attempt to freeze time that fails. He too does not want to "leave this country" yet has no choice when he is “taken by the suck of the sea”. Here the wave of time has taken him. Time cannot be resisted or stopped. It may seem that things are unaffected but this is only an illusion.

The final couplet reinforces this idea with the decay of the gulls. Here, symbolic of all living things, the gulls show that death is both inevitable and remorseless. Time seems not to care as it “flows past them”. Referring back to beginning line of the poem continues the flowing structure of all the sections. Using the cyclic structure the end is firmly tied to the beginning. This structure beautifully reflects the continuum of time.

ANALYSIS – HUMAN EXPERIENCES

As we stated in the opening section,

> Time is a powerful force that sweeps all along toward aging and death. Both these ideas are central to the human experience, both individually and collectively.

'Out of Time' in its three sonnets is an extended metaphor of time as a wave with the water imagery showing relentless progress. In the first sonnet he personifies time with the yacht imagery and then the idea of the wave before finally addressing time directly. In the second he shows us the human experience is affected by time as is all life and we cannot hold back time and in the final sonnet he shows us that a scene will always change no matter how we try and fix it before returning to the cyclical nature of things.

Roderick Heath also states that human experiences in the poem can be seen in this way,

> Consider also in 'Out of Time', where "(t)he moment's world as it was; and I was part / Fleshless and ageless, changeless and was made free." Slessor's concept of freedom seems precisely to invite a boundless disintegration of form, a complete immersion in the totality of things. "The gulls go down, the body dies and rots / And time flows past them like a hundred yachts." The physical world decays, in the relentless march of time. There's no intimation of a god or an afterlife here; it's more as if time itself is the god, neither cruel nor pitying but implacable, that Slessor envisions.
>
> *http://englishoneoworst.blogspot.com.au/2010/03/kenneth-slessor-frozen-moments-of-out.html*

Questions: 'Out of Time'

1. Summarise what happens in this poem in THREE sentences.

2. Choose TWO images Slessor has used in the poem and explain why each is effective.

3. Explain how the structure of the poem helps make a comment about time. In your answer you will need to refer to the sonnet use, the links between sonnets and the repeated images.

4. Slessor uses language to create movement to try and capture the relentless progress of time. Explain how he achieves this by discussing at least THREE language techniques he uses.

5. Analyse Slessor's use of present participles (e.g. 'ing' words) and adverbs (e.g. 'ly' words) has helped represent the movement of time.

6. Explain how the personification important to the representation of time. How does Slessor portray time as central to human experiences?

Extended Writing Task: 'Out of Time'

Argue **either** for **or** against the proposition that this poem is pessimistic in terms of the human experience. How might it be read to prove the opposing argument?

Refer in detail to the ideas, structure and poetic techniques of 'Out of Time'.

WILD GRAPES

Summary

In 'Wild Grapes' Slessor describes a place where time seems to stand still and events and memories from the past are here and part of the present. Here the vivid descriptions of the "old orchard" are drawn from the present but are developed and referenced from lucid memories. The "Isabella grapes" remind the persona of a girl who was there in the orchard in times past. This is a very personal human experience and we can see the persona's motivations for these memories that form a part of how he sees the world.

Glossary

sour	An acid taste like vinegar or lemon
bitter	Harsh, disagreeable taste. Also in the context of this poem it may refer to the hard to bear or distressful feelings that the persona has about his experiences.
dogstars	It is a bright star in Canis Major (Sirius) and in Canis Minor (Procyn). Easily seen.
musket-shot	A musket is a 16th century gun that fired small shot like the grapes in the poem. It shows that the grapes are smallish and under-formed.
lingered	To remain or stay in a place longer than is expected or necessary. Shows a reluctance to leave.
defiant	Resist or challenge.

swallows	Here it refers to a type of bird. The swallows and martins, are a family of birds found around the world on all continents except Antarctica. Highly adapted to aerial feeding, they have a distinctive appearance. There are around 83 species in 19 genera, with the greatest diversity found in Africa, which is also thought to be where they evolved as hole-nesters. They also occur on a number of oceanic islands. A number of European and North American species are long-distance migrants. Within the Old World, the name *martin* tends to be used for the squarer-tailed species, and the name *swallow* for the more fork-tailed species.
bough	Branch of a tree
fierce	Wild, savage and hostile, a violent force.
remembers	Recall in the mind, to retain in the memory.

Analysis

Isabella grapes are a real variety – once very common and often allowed to run wild for shade – but the grapes are bitter and only good for preserving in jams and such. The poem in general is a type of personification of Isabella and the grapes merge as one, especially in the final two lines. It is this construct that gives the poem its resonance with readers – the images around Isabella which form her persona – is what captures the reader's imagination as we wonder about her and the intrigue that seems to surround her and her fate in this orchard. It seems that even Slessor himself was intrigued by the narrative around her.

The poem begins in the "old orchard" and Slessor creates the scene through the use of the senses as he does in so many of the poems set for study. Use of words such as "smoking", "sour", "broken" and "bitter" use the senses to create a feeling of abandonment and illustrate how the ravages of time have affected the orchard and the things that live in it. The memory of the "vanished Mulligans, Or Hartigans" shows that the memory is imperfect, faulty and some things have been lost in the passing of time. The orchard has gone "sour", "boughs" are down and uncleared and no one seems to "care" about the place anymore.

The original men who tended the orchard have long gone, the earth "drowned" both literally and metaphorically. In the past when the orchard had been cared for the fruit was excellent. Slessor writes, the cherries "grew" and the apples were "bright as dogstars". We then get the concept of the Isabella grapes, both as the literal grape and then the girl herself. It is the taste of the grape flesh "half-savage with black fur" that conjures the memory and the "Acid and gipsy-sweet" could refer to both. He states bluntly "Isabella, the dead girl" which immediately raises the question in the audiences mind about the circumstances of this death. This mysterious aspect adds to the concept of time passing and memory. Clearly we would like some definitive form of resolution and this creates an imperative response to read on.

It is though, the grapes that live on "Defiantly". Everything else seems lifeless in an "old orchard" where the "swallows never stir". The persona then dwells on the name Isabella and the grapes and the girl become interwoven in his memories and the oxymoronic "harsh sweetness" of the grapes is also reminiscent of the girl. He gets images of her, "dark hair swinging and silver pins" and yet she is "as these grapes" being "half-fierce, half-melting". This links to the idea that the girl is a gipsy a nomadic, independent and passionate people whose exploits have been narratives for centuries, especially as they live outside of conservative society. Perhaps she was wild like the grapes and we can see the sexual imagery in these final stanzas and the very specific "Kissed here".

Whatever happened to Isabella? The final line suggests that memory is fading with its "-but who remembers now?" The dichotomy of the final line suggests a passionate end with her two-sided personality but also the fact that once we are dead we are forgotten, a fading memory, just like the Hartigans and Mulligans that we see in the first stanza. Obviously he doesn't accurately remember but it is the speculation that makes the poem interesting and gives us something to consider.

When we consider what might have been we need to think in terms of the poem's ambiguity. Nothing is clear and this signifies the sense of memory in the poem as memories are often unclear with the passing of time. The girl, Isabella, becomes seemingly personified as the memories of the grapes and her mix creating a further sense of mystery. The rhyme scheme where the first, second and fifth lines of each stanza rhyme also contribute to this as the sounds blur as the poem progresses from the sighing sound "air" in the first to the "ow" sound in the final stanza.

Slessor builds the mystery behind the poem through the "smoking air" type images that are clearly not strong concrete images but impressions as the persona wanders through his memory in this orchard. The grapes have survived and so has the memory of the girl and here they are interwoven in a melancholy way, perhaps for what might have been or what has been lost.

Now let's have a look at the specifics of how the poem explores human experiences.

ANALYSIS – HUMAN EXPERIENCES

Slessor here focuses on memory and the passing of time – two key ideas in his repertoire. The persona visits an old orchard and this stirs memories which draw on past experiences. It is with a sense of loss he begins these reflections as the orchard has degenerated over time. Perhaps you think here there may be a sense of regret which is a feature of human experience.

The success of the orchard which appears to be initially good, e.g. the "cherries" and "apples", has faded and the sense of loss is palpable. Yet it is more than the physical decline of the orchard in this experience and the girl "Isabella" appears in the third stanza brought on by the sensory taste of the grapes also named Isabella.

The personas experiences are clouded because time has passed and in the end he can't remember "now" the clear conclusion to his knowing her. Despite some loss of memory she has "lingered on" like the grapes and the defiance in her persistence to being erased is like the grapes that have still successfully grown despite everything else, including the people, been "drowned in earth themselves".

The last two stanzas especially have a sense of the sensual imagery conjured by the experiences of the gipsy girl. Her passion and wild nature are clear. We don't get a clear description, rather brief images such as the "dark hair" and "silver pins" with her character "half-fierce, half-melting" suggesting a dichotomy in his remembrances.

It is clear here that not all human experiences are clear over time. Memories fade and the images change. In some ways Slessor suggests that we can never go back. Can we ever be completely clear on anything?

Questions: 'Wild Grapes'

1. Summarise what happens in this poem in THREE sentences.
2. Choose TWO images Slessor has used in the poem and explain why each is effective.
3. Explain how the structure of the poem helps develop the ideas that Slessor is conveying. In your answer you will need to refer to the poem specifically.
4. Slessor uses language to reinforce his ideas. Explain how he achieves this by discussing at least THREE language techniques he uses.
5. Analyse Slessor's near personification of the grapes by interweaving them with the gipsy girl, Isabella. Is this effective in conveying a sense of how memory is inaccurate?
6. Explain how the ambiguity of the poem makes it interesting or, if you think otherwise, ineffective. How does Slessor portray time and memory as central to human experiences?

Extended Writing Task: 'Wild Grapes'

Argue **either** for **or** against the proposition that this poem conveys a sense of regret. How might it be read to prove the opposing argument?

Refer in detail to the ideas, structure and poetic techniques of 'Wild Grapes'.

GULLIVER

Summary

'Gulliver' is a poem that uses a literary allusion to connect the fate of Gulliver to the plight of modern 'man' and the problems we face with living. Slessor wants to escape the mortality of living and in the final line calls the "hangman" as a means of escape from the problems he has listed in the poem.

Glossary

dungeon	A strong, dark cell or prison, usually placed underground
tyranny	Unrestrained use of power, absolute rule used with severity and hardness.
sinews	Tendons in the body
twopenny	An amount of money (twopence), something of very little value or worthless
cur	A mongrel dog but also in this instance a mean, cowardly person
manacles	A handcuff or shackle
entwine	To bind or bring together
neuralgia	A sharp pain along a nerve
spongy	Lacking in firmness or solidarity, being able to absorb as in having a light porous constitution
hangman	A person who hangs criminals who have been condemned to death.

Analysis

'Gulliver' is a modern poem in terms of the human experience and the content and language reflect this. Using a literary analogy to Swift's *Gulliver's Travels* Slessor translates this into a treatise of modern living and the problems associated in it. To set the context Gulliver is the protagonist in Swift's novel Gulliver's Travels and in the first book he travels to Lilliput where,

> The travel begins with a short preamble in which Lemuel Gulliver gives a brief outline of his life and history before his voyages.
>
> During his first voyage, Gulliver is washed ashore after a shipwreck and finds himself a prisoner of a race of tiny people, less than 6 inches (15 cm) tall, who are inhabitants of the island country of Lilliput. After giving assurances of his good behaviour, he is given a residence in Lilliput and becomes a favourite of the Lilliput royal court. He is also given permission by the King of Lilliput to go around the city on condition that he must not harm their subjects.
>
> At first, the Lilliputians are hospitable to Gulliver, but they are also wary of the threat that his size poses to them. The Lilliputians reveal themselves to be a people who put great emphasis on trivial matters. For example, which end of an egg a person cracks becomes the basis of a deep political rift within that nation. They are a people who revel in displays of authority and performances of power. Gulliver assists the Lilliputians to subdue their neighbours, the Blefuscudians, by stealing their fleet. However, he refuses to reduce the island nation of Blefuscu to a province of Lilliput, displeasing the King and the royal court.

Gulliver is charged with treason for, among other crimes, "making water" in the capital though he was putting out a fire and saving countless lives. He is convicted and sentenced to be blinded. With the assistance of a kind friend, "a considerable person at court", he escapes to Blefuscu. Here, he spots and retrieves an abandoned boat and sails out to be rescued by a passing ship, which safely takes him back home.

https://en.wikipedia.org/wiki/Gulliver%27s_Travels

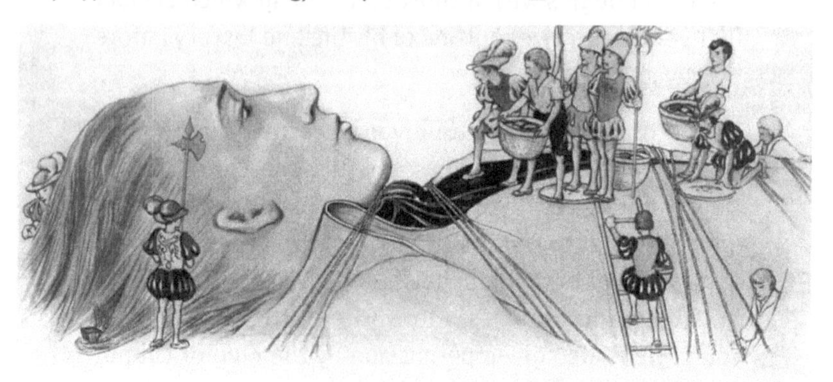

We have seen this sense of ambiguity in some of the other poems set for study and here the impression is that life is a constant struggle against the tribulations that it throws at us. This is especially tied to the physical form and the ageing that time brings. It is an especially personal poem with the beginning "I'll" and the repetition of the "I" constantly throughout the poem. As Slessor tries to escape the "tyranny of sinews" that is his physical form he begins to list the problems of being,

> Lashed with a hundred ropes of nerve and bone

we get the images of his body as a prison that he cannot escape because it isn't a tangible "dungeon" or "manacles" or "cage" that he can remove himself from. The problems are the "hair"(s) of the little things that stop us and with a solution to each one "ten thousand" come to "entwine" him. Slessor begins to list some of our human experiences,

> Love, hunger, drunkenness, neuralgia, debt,
> Cold weather, hot weather, sleep and age –

He asks, "But who ever heard of a cage of hairs?" and again in the penultimate line asks a similar question. The problems of life are insoluble hence the use of these rhetorical questions. His only solution seems to be death as he calls for the "hangman". This is a culmination of all the prison imagery as if life is a jail and the only escape is the hangman as all other alternatives have been lost.

Analysis – Human Experiences

Slessor gives us a bleak or realistic view depending on your point of view on the human experience. He lists what he sees as human experiences in the text that make our lives burdensome and he is sufficiently emotive to be 'sobbing' with frustration at his situation. Remember this is not just Slessor but he is speaking for 'everyone' that might read the poem or indeed everyone who has existed. He says of his own experience,

> It is difficult for any writer to discuss his own verse, mainly because of the problem of deciding where the boundary lies between the personal associations and meanings which certain words produce in him and those which they produce in the reader. In any case, the very act of analysing emotional documents composed twenty or thirty years ago is often impossible for the author – he may feel that he is in the position of a palaeontologist asked to report on a specimen of fossilised fern.
>
> (*Kenneth Slessor Selected Poems* p. 130)

Judith Wright the famous Australian poet has said of Gulliver,

> [In 'Gulliver'] Slessor probably discovered the most precise and eloquent image of the plight of modern man that Australian poetry is ever likely to produce.

This is the most eloquent analysis of how Slessor's poem touches human experiences and the things that restrain and bind us in the modern, mortal world. He is "poor helpless Gulliver" and asks us where we stand. Is this the truth about human experiences or too pessimistic for most?

Questions: 'Gulliver'

1. Summarise what happens in this poem in THREE sentences.
2. Choose TWO images Slessor has used in the poem and explain why each is effective.
3. Explain how the prison imagery helps convey the ideas on human experiences that Slessor is trying to convey.
4. Slessor uses language to reinforce his ideas. Explain how he achieves this by discussing at least THREE language techniques he uses.
5. Analyse why Slessor makes this poem so personal with the use of "I" and "I'll" repeatedly?
6. Explain how the ambiguity of the poem makes it interesting or, if you think otherwise, ineffective. How does Slessor portray ageing and life as central to human experiences?

Extended Writing Task: 'Gulliver'

Argue **either** for **or** against the proposition that this poem conveys a sense of complete helplessness in the face of a remorseless modern life. How might it be analysed to show the opposite?

Refer in detail to the ideas, structure and poetic techniques of 'Gulliver'.

VESPER-SONG OF THE REVEREND SAMUEL MARSDEN

Summary

The poem is a study of the Reverend Samuel Marsden and in it he reveals his true self rather than the historical figure that is seen in a more positive light as an early Australian pioneer. In the poem we see the hypocrisy of the religious figure as it is contrasted with his views of flogging convicts and his real attitude toward them.

Glossary

brutes Brutal, insensitive or cruel person. An individual with animal qualities, non-human

tainted A trace or part that is contaminated or offensive, discredited

welt A ridge or raised spot on the body as a result of a blow from a whip or stick

sacramental Relates to the sacrament, the Eucharist or the Lord's Supper in a religious sense. Simplified it can be the bread eaten at the communion.

knout A whip with a lash of leather used for flogging criminals

vileness Highly offensive, wretched and bad. A character who is offensive or objectionable to the senses or feelings

litany A ceremonial form of prayer. Recited prayer or a repetition of responses that are called for in a church service.

weal	Wealth or riches, prosperity and happiness. Not commonly used now.
vellum	A skin, usually calf or lamb that can be treated for use as a writing surface, a manuscript
scourged	A whip or lash used for the causing of pain in punishment, a cause of a problem, to punish
overseer	A supervisor or manager
wretch	An unfortunate or unhappy person, someone of poor character

Analysis

A Companion to Australian Literature Since 1900 says the poem is "an unflattering portrait of a founding white Antipodean". Les Murray the Australian poet says of Marsden in an interview,

> Yeah Sam Marsden was the, I don't know what his actual title was, but he was a kind of missionary cleric of Sydney. The kind of dominating ecclesiastical bully of the age... Total hypocrite of course because he was dealing in the guns with the Maoris at the same time. Where the Maoris got silver to buy guns with I don't know but at least they knew it was going to cost money. He never sold anything to the aborigines cause they had nothing to give him.
>
> *https://www.uts.edu.au/file/31441/transcript*

A detailed biography of the man can be found at

http://adb.anu.edu.au/biography/marsden-samuel-2433

The Wikipedia entry is also detailed and kinder than Murray's summation but has this quick precis,

> Samuel Marsden (25 June 1765 – 12 May 1838) was an English born Anglican cleric and a prominent member of the Church Missionary Society, believed to have introduced Christianity to New Zealand.
>
> Marsden was a prominent figure in early New South Wales and Australian history, partly through his ecclesiastical offices as the colony's senior Anglican cleric, but also for his employment of convicts for farming and his actions as a magistrate at Parramatta, both of which attracted contemporary criticism.

Slessor wrote about Australia but not the bushman imagery and he certainly didn't mythologise the past as some poets have done. This poem goes to the hypocrisy and cynicism that underlay much of early Australian society. Marsden is a conflicting figure in Australian history and under Governor Hunter he was recognised as a man who wanted to save souls for God but he was also a magistrate and had to punish convicts he was attempting to 'save'. He had men flogged mercilessly and often in hope of confession. He was a high-minded man who detested the morality and ethics of convicts. He believed discipline (physical punishment) was the best method of getting order.

This is the man Slessor captures in the poem, the focus of the poem is on the man's personality and it as if Marsden is addressing his congregation or 'audience' and this highlights the conflict between the two. His sense of ownership of the convicts is expressed in the opening line,

> MY cure of souls, my cage of brutes,

And reinforced by his attitude toward them in the second line,

> Go lick and learn at these my boots!

While in the final line Marsden calls himself a "humble wretch" it is ironic when you consider how he views himself in the previous lines where he calls on "God's leather" to beat the convicts into submission with some vivid descriptions of the floggings he would give them. You may well need the glossary provided as many of the terms Slessor uses are archaic and may be unfamiliar to you. He has used this language to make the 'Song' more realistic and shows us the thinking of Marsden. Marsden thinks he can "cure" the souls of men in this initial pun (see the term curate) with this "sacramental knout".

We see a plethora of religious words and images as you would expect from a reverend but the terminology is twisted for his purposes and perspective. The use of religious terms in a violent way seems odd to the reader and the hypocritical use of the term "glory" is intriguing as he claims to use the term for God but we get the impression it is all about Marsden's glory. In fact the religious terms make up about a third of the poem as you would expect from a 'Vesper-Song' yet we get no real sense of religion, rather an analysis of the man.

What Slessor does in the poem is to give the audience a vicious critique of Samuel Marsden. This is a poem Slessor wrote on the anniversary of Marsden's death when he was being celebrated as a pioneer. Slessor doesn't like what Marsden represents and finds his religious piety hypocritical in contrast to the concept of the magistrate. In fact Marsden appears to thrive on his cruelty and he cites his view of the floggings in terms "blood" and "meat" in a near sadistic manner.

Analysis – Human Experiences

Jonathan Foye (2016) writes in an analysis of Anglican ministry in the Sydney district about Marsden,

> Historical opinion on the Church of England's second chaplain to the colony of New South Wales, the Reverend Samuel Marsden, varies. In Australia he is renowned as a brutal 'flogging parson' who, while serving as a Parramatta Magistrate up until his unceremonious removal in 1822, inflicted unusually harsh punishments for even the most minor of infractions. A popular Australian saying concerning Marsden was that, "he sentences the prisoner on the Saturday, admonishes him on Sunday and flogs him on Monday" (Porter, 2006: 35). On the other hand, Marsden has a far gentler reputation in New Zealand. There he is remembered for his ministry to the Māori and widely regarded as having introduced sheep to the nation (Yarwood, 1996: xi).
>
> *http://researchdirect.uws.edu.au/islandora/object/uws%3A34085/datastream/PDF/view*

It is true that he is a conflicting figure and this is what Slessor expresses in the poem. This is what the human experience is though. Marsden thought sincerely he was doing the right thing and yet in a later perspective we can see the anomalies of his behaviour. At the time and even much later he was seen as a fine figure in Australian colonial history, a man who wanted order and also to save the souls of the convicts.

We can see here that assumptions about people's behaviour and motivations may change with time and context. We certainly have contrasting visions of Marsden and even as you read this debate continues about his position historically. The poem indicates Slessor's perspective clearly and he gives us a very emotional response by allowing Marsden to speak for himself and elucidate his feelings about the convicts and the punishments they need to get to heaven.

What this poem shows us is that human experiences may change with time and may not always be clear and certain. People have anomalies in their behaviour and these may come from beliefs and/ or emotional responses. These may not always become clear, even in perspective and we may also bring our own prejudices into the analysis. This truly represents human experiences. We can also consider here how the convicts may have felt about his ideas and the physical experiences as expressed by Slessor can't have been positive.

Questions: 'Vesper-Song of the Reverend Samuel Marsden'

1. Summarise what happens in this poem in THREE sentences.
2. Choose TWO images Slessor has used in the poem and explain why each is effective.
3. Explain how the structure of the poem helps develop the ideas that Slessor is conveying. In your answer you will need to refer to the poem specifically.
4. Slessor uses archaic language to reinforce his ideas. Explain how he achieves this by discussing THREE specific terms.
5. Analyse Slessor's view of Marsden. Is it accurate from your reading of the poem and other sources or has he been too harsh?
6. Explain how the ambiguity of the poem makes it interesting or, if you think otherwise, ineffective. How does Slessor portray time and memory as central to human experiences?

Extended Writing Task: 'Vesper-Song of the Reverend Samuel Marsden'

Argue **either** for **or** against the proposition that this poem is a realistic portrayal of an historical figure in terms of human experiences.

Refer in detail to the ideas, structure and poetic techniques of 'Vesper-Song of the Reverend Samuel Marsden'.

WILLIAM STREET

Summary

'William Street' is a four stanza poem representing his later work and published in 1939. In the poem he takes a real scene (William Street in Kings Cross, Sydney) and recreates it. This recreation can be read on two levels and both are valid in our study of the poem. The first is where the reader can experience the sensual images his poetry is known for but also the feelings and emotions they conjure. The second is a more symbolic meaning and in this poem it is his defence of the fascinations of the city which are relevant for this study.

Glossary

pulsing	The regular throbbing or rhythmic recurrence of vibrations
dangle	To hang loosely with a jerking or swaying motion
suffer	To have a feeling of pain or distress, injury or loss
condemn	To express an unfavourable judgement, strongly disapprove, to judge
rasping	Harsh and/or grating
paraffin	A white colourless, tasteless substance made from petroleum that was and is used in candles, sealing and waterproofing.
crimp	To press into small regular folds

dips	Slang term for pick-pocket from the act of dipping (taking) something.
molls	Archaic term for prostitute
pasturage	A piece of ground used for grazing livestock

Analysis

Slessor wrote of 'William Street' that it was "a sort of flashlight photograph of the swarming city channel that runs up the hill of Kings Cross, taken on a rainy night when the surface of the road is coated with a slick (of colours) from neon". These colours are the "red globes", "liquor green" and "pulsing arrows" of the first stanza. These visual images are the meat of the first stanza. The realism of the reflected lights takes on a more primitive feel with Slessor as the persona pointing out "running fire, Spilt on stones". This sacrificial image goes to a more vital kind of life that we find in the city- the vitality of desperation we see in the characters at the end of the poem. This concept is supported by the continual movement in the poem e.g. "pulsing" and the more natural image of the "stream" which is an unusual word in such a cityscape. This for Slessor is beautiful and this is his theme and concern, he does "find it lovely".

Even with the darker images of the second and final stanzas the poet still finds something positive to find "lovely". In the second stanza images of "Ghost's trousers" and "hung men" are seen in pawnshop windows. These second hand clothes have no body in them "to suffer or condemn". This is an important point as Slessor sees the beauty but makes no moral comment on anything in the poem- he is the observer and he likes what he sees.

The third stanza returns the reader to the more sensuous image of the smells "rich and rasping". Clear and descriptive here he lists a catalogue of smells that give the area its own feel and texture. They are strong smells and the alliteration of the 's' sound gives the sense of cooking oil in a vat in a Greek café. Here again the alliteration within phrases e.g. "rich and rasping", "puffs of paraffin" give a sense of rhythm making the scene more immediate. The poet also returns to the religious imagery of the first stanza with the language of "blesses" contrasting with the "hiss" of the snake. This kind of contrast is used in much of Slessor's work and can be used as a link between the poems.

The final stanza deals with the people that inhabit William Street. The "dips" (pickpockets) and "molls" (prostitutes) are living a real and vital existence with "death" and "hunger". They do not walk the street but "range the pavement" like wild animals. These dark images are central to the contrast again in that repetitive line "You find it ugly, I find it lovely". Slessor uses the full extent of his poetic technique in this brief and complex poem. The ambivalent images are created not only by his description and feelings about the city but by the language.

Slessor wrote of the language in 'William Street' "I have attempted to create a neon lit, metallic and floozy atmosphere by the deliberate use of assonance... I have rhymed in this way such words as "green" and "stream" and "men" and "condemn". 'William Street' is a carefully crafted poem of the city and what it offers to the keen and non-judgmental observer."

Analysis – Human Experiences

Since Slessor wrote the poem 'William Street' has changed significantly and while it still may be worth having a look through something like Google Earth much of the 'life' has gone from the area, especially after the Baird liberal government brought in its no drinking laws which curtailed the nightlife of the area. Prior to this William Street and surrounds had a reputation for covering most of the human experiences with its strip clubs, bars and its reputation for drugs and prostitution. It also had a bohemian lifestyle and was home to many creative types, especially in Slessor's time there.

Slessor in his 'A Portrait of Sydney' reprinted in *Bread and Wine* (p14-15) says of Kings Cross,

> ...with its unending flux of lights, its gaudiness and its reticence, its sunsets and midnights, it seems (to me) a good deal more beautiful than the highly advertised stones and sand of Central Australia. To me, the Chevron Hilton hotel, with its glittering windows and huge verticals, is as awe inspiring as Ayer's Rock (now called Uluru – ed)...the Cross itself is perpetually expressing a state of mind.

Slessor is fascinated by the city and the people in it, the environment created by the inhabitants, the landscape that give it so much of its humanity. When we examine how he sees these people and view the experiences they and he has we see a vital living thing. For our poet-guide we have a view that is not conventionally moral, Slessor here is not a judge of human nature he just sees it for what it is. He doesn't criticise he enables us to see it for what it is, perhaps an ambivalent scene – and isn't that what the human experience is?

Specifically through each of the stanzas we get glimpses of life from the wet streets, through the pawnshop to the eateries that dot the streetscape. Slessor doesn't hide the poverty, the down on their luck individuals, the criminals, the whores but sees the beauty within each of their experiences. Despite this he does see the ambivalence in human existence and notes clearly,

> You find it ugly, I find it lovely.

I think the purpose of the poem is to convey the complexities of human experiences and that we should appreciate them rather than be moralistic or judgemental. It is not just a description of humanity it is symbolic of defending and celebrating life, especially the city life at a time when the bush was seen as central to the Australian identity. There is energy in the city, pushed forward by the sensory images he creates and the individuals themselves which offer promises of personal narratives amidst the sea of experiences available. This speaks directly to human experiences.

Questions: 'William Street'

1. Summarise what happens in this poem in THREE sentences.
2. Choose TWO images Slessor has used in the poem and explain why each is effective.
3. Explain how Slessor argues for the 'lovely' aspects of the city. In your answer you will need to refer to the poem specifically and the images he uses.
4. Slessor uses language to create the sensual images that convey the different aspects of the city. Explain how he achieves this by discussing at least THREE language techniques he uses in 'William Street'.

5. Analyse Slessor's use of the senses in the poem and the effectiveness of ONE of the sensory images he uses.

6. Explain how Slessor conveys city life as central to the human experiences he shows and despite the dark images the poem is surprisingly positive.

Extended Writing Task: 'William Street'

Argue **either** for **or** against the idea that 'William Street' succeeds in its premise that the city is 'lovely' despite the ugliness one might find there.

Refer in detail to the poem.

BEACH BURIAL

Summary

This is a sad, moving poem which tells of the bodies of soldiers dead in war. The soldiers are rolling in the surf and being washed up on the beaches. They are without identities and each is buried as an "unknown seaman" irrespective of what side they were on. The dead are joined "on the other front", in death. Different people see the poem as about different things. It has been thought of as an anti-war poem, a Christian poem, even a poem about death and the bonds of humanity. You need to decide what you see as its main ideas.

Glossary

Gulf of Arabs	Refers to the Arabian Gulf which has also been called the Red Sea and Persian Gulf
convoy	A group of ships or vehicles that are accompanied by an escort for protection and travelling in the same direction
tidewood	Wood that has been washed to shore by the tide
perplexity	The state of being uncertain about a situation
bewildered	Confused and perplexed

inscription	A brief dedication
landfall	The approach or sighting of land
enlisted	To enter the Armed Forces. Here it means the individual has joined the 'other front' being death

Analysis

The poem is thought of as an elegy as it is a lament for the dead soldiers lost near El Alamein on the Arabian Gulf, a battle fought in World War Two in the Middle East. Australians were involved and, at the time, Australians would have been closely monitoring the events. Slessor was a war correspondent in the area and was moved by the events as he saw them.

His reference to the specific battle site at the conclusion of the poem has a number of effects. It establishes the reality of the situation and also would have presented a very different view to the general triumph and heroism that was associated with the battle. Those who see the poem as an anti-war text are quick to note this. Slessor's understated poem rejects melodrama, instead developing into a poignant argument against the dehumanisation and waste of war.

The poem's title begins this calm, sombre approach. It is not overly emotional and hardly readies us for the sadness of the poem. The first stanza begins quietly and quickly establishes a grave atmosphere. The tone is sad and the pace is slow. It has been said to sound like a funeral march. The use of present tense gives the events immediacy and emphasises the continuous nature of the events described.

This poem is celebrated for its use of sound techniques. The assonance and alliteration in:

> At night they sway and wander in the waters far under

recreates perfectly the slow rocking of the bodies in the water. The next line,

> But morning rolls them in the foam

is a sharp contrast of energetic movement which mirrors the bodies coming up on the beach. The use of "But" emphasises this difference. It is also important that the bodies are nameless. They are referred to impersonally as "they" and "them" while the term "dead bodies" is coldly precise. An atmosphere of sad pity is created. The dead are powerless and at the mercy of the water. You might parallel this to their lack of influence in the war they fought. It is hard to reconcile this image any glorious or triumphant image of war.

The second stanza tells of the burial of the dead. Again the scene is aurally recreated. The "sob and clubbing of the gunfire" is cleverly like the sound of distant weaponry. Yet beyond the actual sounds, the ironic disparity between shooting that both cries ("sobs") and kills brutally ("clubbing") is an effective image to extend the sense of tragic loss and the incongruous nature of war.

Equally anonymous is the burier of the dead - "Someone, it seems, has time for this". There is a tone of incredulity with the "seems". The burial is crude and makeshift. The pace of the procedure is mimicked by the rhythm and pace of,

> To pluck them from the shallows and bury them in burrows
> And tread the sand upon their nakedness

It is a process which reveals it has been done many times before. This implies great losses in war. The vulnerability of the dead is emphasised by their "nakedness".

The cross for each grave is rough and makeshift "tidewood". The use of the word "driven" has connotations of force and violence that reminds us of the horror these men have endured – in life and death. The crosses bear the "last signature", supposedly an individual's name and mark, but ironically there is no individual signature – they are all equally the same. The repetition of "such" in

> Written with such perplexity, with such bewildered pity

stresses the incomprehensible situation. The futile waste of life and the inhumane treatment of people by war is represented by these crosses and the impermanence of any writing upon them.

The men may well have died for nothing. The hyphen at the end of the line, "The words choke as they begin-" aurally represents the inability to speak further. The pain restricts speech.

Not only are they only covered by sand but the crude nature of their burial is also shown by their rough, quite unsatisfactory, headstones. There is no individuality, no identity – instead they are each "Unknown seaman". The water's effect on the ink makes "a ghostly pencil" that "Wavers and fades, the purple drips". Slessor uses this to highlight the dehumanisation of war and create very negative connotations. The simile, "As blue as dead men's lips", likens the running ink to the dead men's appearance and is particularly ghastly. It is intended to shock the audience. It is clear the persona is not uninvolved but sees the events as distressing and horrifying.

The final stanza is often seen to show Slessor's more general concerns beyond simple anti-war sentiments.

Here it is shown that these bodies are from both sides in the war, and even those who were not directly involved. The line, "gone in search of the same landfall", refers to all soldiers' goal of victory, irrespective of who they fight for. They are united by these hopes and aspirations. Ironically, even if they were opposed, they were joined by this and their eventual death.

> ...the sand joins them together,
> Enlisted on the other front.

Literally they are joined through their proximity in the "burrows" but figuratively they are joined by death.

Some have seen this as a Christian message of being united in Heaven despite Slessor's professed atheism. They would see the poem to use Christian images such as the cross and the concept of sacrifice.

Others have seen the final stanza as showing that in 'Beach Burial' Slessor was concerned more generally with humankind, not so much war. Here the image of being united in death is seen to symbolise the bonds of humanity. People may deny their relationship with other cultures by making war upon them but we are all linked by the human condition. The links are shown by the compassion of the grave digger and the irony that death effectively makes any dispute in war irrelevant. Slessor himself promoted this reading by saying:

> The superficial meaning, of course, is a military one. The verses were written at a time when there was pressure on the allies to open a 'second front' against the Germans.
>
> However, there is a deeper implication which is really the theme of the poem. It is the idea that all men of all races, whether they fight with each other or not, are engaged together on the common 'front' of humanity's existence. The absolute fact of death unites them. Their hatreds, quarrels and wars should be dwarfed by the huger human struggle to survive against disease and cataclysms on this dangerous planet.[1]

The bonds of humanity are symbolised by the joining in death through burial. You might see Slessor as saying life should go beyond futile wars.

---

1 From 'Some Notes on the Poems' in *Selected Poems* (Angus and Robertson, Sydney, 1975)

Many people do not see the poem this way and, even though Slessor says this, you do not have to agree with him. There are plenty of composers who disagree with their audience's perception of their work. It is essential you can defend your reading by closely referring to many different aspects of the text. For instance, if you really think it is an anti-war poem, you might think a few lines at the end is not really enough to move the poem's focus away from the sense of loss. If you see it as about humanity, you need to see where else this is implied in the poem. What about the title?

Other people have seen the notion of death as the main idea. They see that Slessor's idea of inevitable death and our powerlessness to stop it is shown in the poem. Here death is the common experience of all races and perhaps can be seen to be far more potent than any conflict man can create. The imagery of the sea and the rolling waves is important as seen in other poems.

Analysis – Human Experiences

Here we see that Slessor covers many of the aspects of the human experience not just death and the issues surrounding war, although these are primary for most audiences. It is true that Slessor uses the war as a prime factor but he also allows us to examine our own responses to many of the questions he raises. The poem itself comes from Slessor's direct experience and in his appendix to *Selected Poems* he wrote,

> In the morning it was not uncommon to find the bodies of drowned men washed up on the beaches. They were buried in the sandhills under improvised crosses, identification being usually impossible. Most of them were sailors, some British, some German or Italian, some of them 'neutrals'.

Slessor here questions the mythology of war and the concept of heroics. Death is a neutral thing; it doesn't discriminate and is the common experience that binds all humanity. He describes the deaths as a waste and implies that we would be better using the emotions and energies in helping humanity. The experiences of the soldiers must teach us something and the powerful emotions that Slessor finds within himself and gives in the poem is indicative of this.

Human experiences aren't always positive and here Slessor shows us this through the deaths of others. These men are joined by death and the ideologies they represented mean nothing. Slessor shows us through the final stanza that we are all linked as people, with similar experiences, and this is what is central to the human condition.

Questions: 'Beach Burial'

1. Summarise what this poem is about in THREE sentences.
2. Explain the persona's attitude towards the dead bodies.
3. The poem uses a number of contrasting images. Choose TWO of the following and explain how these contribute to the main idea as you see it.
   - night and day
   - water and the firm sand
   - pride and humility
   - life and death
   - gentleness and violence
4. How does the structure of this poem help represent its main ideas? (look at the regular line lengths, the resonant rhyme scheme by echoing half rhymes...)
5. Slessor uses language to recreate the situation he is describing. Explain how he achieves this with aural techniques.
6. Slessor uses language to recreate the situation he is describing. Explain how he achieves this with imagery.
7. Analyse the aspects of human experiences Slessor explores in this poem.

Extended Writing Task: 'Beach Burial'

'Beach Burial' is a powerful poem but it has caused some dispute among different audiences.

Explain your personal response to the poem and how considering other audiences' responses has helped shape this response.

It is essential you present a strong argument that shows your understanding of human experiences he conveys.

Refer in detail to the ideas, structure and poetic techniques of the poem.

From Newsreel film footage of El Alamein

IDEAS

When we look at Slessor's work in general as pieces that give glimpses into human experiences we can get some very different perspectives. We have given you specifics for each of the poems set for study but there are other ideas which you can integrate into these ideas as a general overview. For example we have listed some of the key ideas in Slessor's work and you can integrate these into the specific ideas. This may help to bind your essay together.

Different people see Slessor's work from different perspectives. Five ideas about human experiences that emerge strongly are:

- Time
- Death
- Memories
- Sensuality / Feelings
- Wasting Life / War

It is important to realise that these are not necessarily distinct ideas. They overlap. You need to decide what the main messages are that you receive from the poetry. You may relate a number of these or come up with something entirely of your own. It will help to step back and think how Slessor feels about life. He definitely sees much of beauty and enjoys the sensual. Yet he has been accused of not really enjoying life and having disgust for its transience.

This means, despite the joy he feels he is angered and appalled over the effects of time as we will all decline and die. I am not at all sure that is the message he wants us to take. I think there is too much beauty and enjoyment. Perhaps instead he wants us to appreciate our weapons against time, memories and sleep, even though they cannot stop time. I'd like to think it is wasting our lives, like in 'Beach Burial'. The ideas below have been discussed at length in the analysis of each poem so I will just make some connections between poems here with some references to human experiences.

If we think, as I have mentioned previously, about the ambivalence in some of his work it is helpful to consider this quote from Noel Rowe in Modern Australian Poets,

> If it is helpful to say that Slessor's poetry is ambivalent, it may also be helpful to imagine the poetry as the window, the glass on which is written the space between life with all its senses and memories, and the dark night of death and nothing (p2)

This is Slessor's view of human experiences and these ideas are interwoven into that.

Time

Slessor's concern with time and its effects runs through most of the poems set for study although the poems.

Overall, Slessor is very aware that time continues and will move past us whether we want it to or not. This puts the notion of humanity's dominance in perspective. Ultimately, we may think we are powerful and controlling our world but our existence is a mere blink in time. Time is incessant and moves on despite the human desire to live.

Time is powerful as depicted cleverly by the poem 'Wild Grapes' where Slessor shows us that time has ravaged the orchard and also the memories of the persona. We are all faced by this and memories are our reminders of the human experiences that we have. Slessor shows us here that these reflections can be vague and even melancholic as we progress in life and age. The experiences shown here are tinged with a sense of loss, both the orchard and the girl, Isabella, have been lost. Time can bring a sense of regret and we see in 'Wild Grapes' that the initial success of 'man' through the original orchardists have been lost in the abandoned orchard which has returned to nature except for the defiant Isabella grapes.

Time also impacts on us in 'Gulliver' where the passing of time just brings problems to us. We also see it obviously in 'Out of Time' where time is a powerful force that sweeps all along toward aging and death. Both these ideas are central to the human experience, both individually and collectively. In 'William Street' we can also see the passing of time through the constant stream of people and the events that Slessor describes.

Death

Slessor explores death in many of his poems. This is a natural link to his concern with time. If we accept that time moves on relentlessly then death is inevitable. It is the natural part of our life-cycle. The poems set for study show this clearly.

Yet there seems no Christian interpretation of death as judgement or as the next stage in eternal life. Slessor was an atheist and his presentation of death is more final.

One of the most interesting ideas about death is in 'Beach Burial' where death is seen to unite humanity. Here Slessor seeks to remind us that all worldly concerns are dwarfed by the inevitable. Human conquests and war are insignificant in death. Many believe Slessor uses the death of the men as a comment about the universality of experience and the pointlessness of war. In death all conflicts are made irrelevant and ironically, resolved.

We can also see this sense of loss in 'Wild Grapes' where "Isabella" is either,

> Kissed here – or killed here – but who remembers now?

This poem is more ambiguous than 'Beach Burial' and yet the sensual experiences of people are reinforced by the images he uses, similar to the emotive imagery in the war poem. His focus on death is also featured when he discusses the 'vanished Mulligans, Or Hartigans' who have 'long drowned in earth themselves'.

Memories

Memories feature in many of the set poems. Memories are presented as strong and forceful in Slessor's poetry. In 'Beach Burial' it is a memory of Slessor's time on the battlefield that inspired the poem.

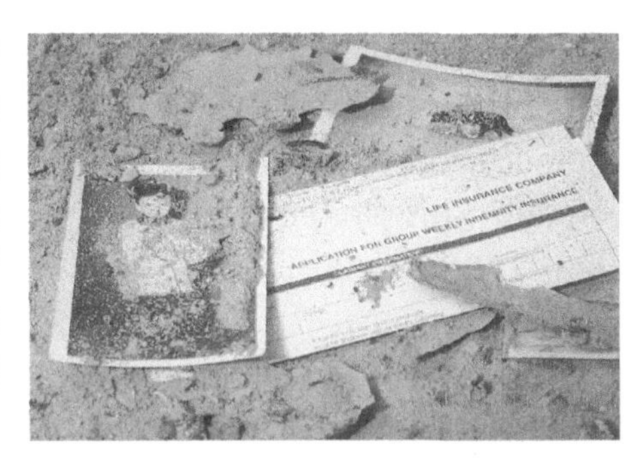

The memories Slessor shows are also fragmented and imprecise as shown in 'Wild Grapes' where the persona states 'but who remembers now?' 'William Street' too shows us how Slessor draws on his memories and reflections on Kings Cross to develop his ideas on the cityscape. Here he examines vignettes of city living along William Street to argue that the city has as much to offer as the countryside and certainly a life of its own. Slessor's memories show the ambiguity of human experience over time and the way we can interpret different perspectives in 'Vesper-Song of the Reverend Samuel Marsden'.

Slessor's very images in the poetry conjure memories and draw us into the poetic experience. What memories do they dredge up from your mind as you read?

Sensuality / Feelings

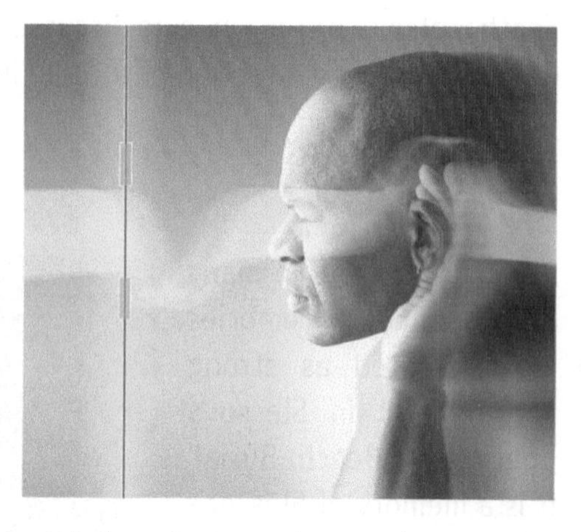

Slessor has been called a "poet of the senses" which means he is a poet who works to use the five senses in his work to evoke feelings and responses in the audience. You know this through his effective aural techniques and tactile images. You have analysed his images and descriptions that seek to evoke atmosphere and recreate feeling. These have been referred to in every poem set for study. His interest in poetic technique shows his pleasure in the senses.

The celebration of the senses is most obviously shown in 'William Street'. Here Slessor writes with passion of the feelings and sensations that are revealed by the machinations of the city, even if some of these are negative. Slessor has attested that sensations are a gift of life.

Many argue that while Slessor is certainly aware of the forces of time and death, his appreciation of the sensual shows us that life is worth living despite the negatives. They see his work as a balancing act where he expresses his concern about life's limitations but uses such richness of language and form that he also celebrates it. You can also find examples of this in each of the poems set for study. Don't forget that emotions are a central concept in explaining human experiences.

Wasting life / War

'Beach Burial' may lead you to decide Slessor is concerned with opposing war. However, this concern is not really seen directly in the other poems set for study.

You might like to step back and think of the implications his criticisms that seem fairly obvious in 'Beach Burial'. For instance, is it the waste of lives that he objects to? Why? You might see Slessor as opposing the dead men's inability to appreciate the world since their lives have been taken from them. This is a little bit like what time does to humans – it too takes us from this world. You might see this as similar to 'Out of Time' when the persona recalls,

> "Fool, would you leave this country?" cried my heart,
> But I was taken by the suck of the sea.

Despite our yearnings to stay and enjoy life, time is relentless and moves along without us. Here war is a bit like time. It takes us with out concern for our individuality or wishes. The dehumanisation and lack of recognition for individuality in war is clearly represented in 'Beach Burial'. Remember the signatures on the crosses and the use of impersonal language.

THE ESSAY

The essay consists of the basic form of an introduction, body paragraphs and conclusion. The esssay has been the subject of numerous texts and you should have the basic form well in hand. As teachers, the point we would emphasise would be to link the paragraphs both to each other and back to your argument (which should directly respond to the question). Of course, ensure your argument is logical and sustained.

Make sure you use specific examples and that your quotes are accurate. To ensure that you respond to the question, make sure you plan carefully and are sure what relevant point each paragraph is making. It is solid technique to actually 'tie up' each point by explicitly coming back to the question.

When composing an essay the basic conventions of the form are:

- State your argument, outline the points to be addressed and perhaps have a brief definition.

↓

A solid structure for each paragraph is:

- Topic sentence (*the main idea and its link to the previous paragraph/ argument*)
- Explanation/ discussion of the point including links between texts if applicable.
- Detailed evidence (*Close textual reference - quotes, incidents and technique discussion.*)
- Tie up by restating the point's relevance to argument/ question

↓

- Summary of points
- Final sentence that restates your argument

As well as this basic structure, you will need to focus on:

Audience – for the essay the audience must be considered formal unless specifically stated otherwise. Therefore, your language must reflect the audience. This gives you the opportunity to use the jargon and vocabulary that you have learnt in English. For the audience ensure your introduction is clear and has impact. Avoid slang or colloquial language including contractions (like 'doesn't', 'e.g.', 'etc.').

Purpose – the purpose of the essay is to answer the question given. The examiner evaluates how well you can make an argument and understand the module's issues and its text(s). An essay is solidly structured so its composer can analyse ideas. This is where you earn marks. It does not retell the story or state the obvious.

Communication – Take a few minutes to plan the essay. If you rush into your answer it is almost certain you will not make the most of the brief 40 minutes to show all you know about the question. More likely you will include irrelevant details that do not gain you marks but waste your precious time. Remember an essay is formal so **do not** do the following: story-tell, list and number points, misquote, use slang or colloquial language, be vague, use non-sentences or fail to address the question.

PLAN:

Don't even think about starting without one!

Introduce...

the texts you are using in the response

Argument: The human experience is affected by:

- Idea One
- Idea Two
- Idea Three

You need to let the marker know what texts you are discussing. You can start with a definition but it can come in the first paragraph of the body. You MUST state your argument in response to the question and the points you will cover as part of it. Wait until the end of the response to give it!

↓

Idea One – Aspect of human experience as outlined in the textual material, e.g. physical impact.

Idea Two – Another aspect of human experience as outlined in the textual material, e.g. psychological impact.

- explain the idea
- where and how is it shown in the prescribed text?
- where and how is it shown in related text 1?

Idea Three – People's sense of experience is affected by context and environment

- explain the idea
- where and how shown in the prescribed text?
- where and how shown in related text 1?

You can use the things you have learned to organise the essay. For each one, you say where you saw this in your prescribed text and where in related text(s).

Two or three ideas are usually enough as you can explore them in detail.

↓

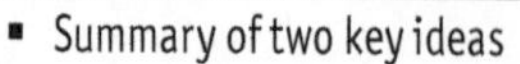

- Summary of two key ideas
- Final sentence that restates your argument

Make sure your conclusion restates your argument. It does not have to be too long.

MODEL ESSAY OUTLINE

To what extent are human experiences significant in the set text?

From your studies respond to this question using your set text and at ONE piece of other textual material

This essay needs to be attacked in a manner that responds to the question and shows ALL your knowledge about the text. The question lends itself to a close study of the poetry of Kenneth Slessor as the text does show how the human experience is integral to life and how it shapes our other experiences and interaction with the world.

An introduction might be written:

> Human experiences are important in Slessors' poetry and the two related texts Lawrence's film *Jindabyne* and Ed Sheeran's song *Castle on the Hill*. These texts show how human experiences are integral to human existence and bring more meaning to one's life. Life is about experiences that challenge us and define how we see the world. They shape our beliefs and attitudes and can be confronting at the same time. Without experiences our lives would be empty and meaningless.

Your essay should then follow the outlined plan and develop these ideas. This gives you the opportunity to link the texts and fully develop each of the ideas.

ANNOTATED RELATED MATERIAL: DIFFERENT STUDIES OF HUMAN EXPERIENCES

Jindabyne – Ray Lawrence

Jindabyne is an Australian film that captures a wide array of human experiences. It touches on the ideas mentioned in the introduction to this text in a number of detailed instances. We can begin by considering the following before beginning a detailed examination of the narrative.

The collective human experience:

- Aboriginality and the spiritual;
- The Fishermen and their code;
- The reaction of the townsfolk;
- Media response;
- Interaction with the natural world.

Individual Experience:

- An individual character's response to the body – choose one;
- The killer;
- Response to the revelations;
- Past experiences and how they impact on current experiences;
- Reaction to loss – emotional;
- Assumptions about life.

We can now look at the plot to help us understand each of these issues. *Jindabyne* begins with the sound of a radio being tuned and the Australian feel of the movie is immediate with the theme music for the ABC news. Lawrence emphasises the isolation by having the radio not tune in correctly for an unknown female character, forcing her to use the cassette player. With this unusual beginning we know that her experience is not going to be positive.

We then pan to the rocks slowly where Gregory, our killer, sits patiently in a truck with the engine running watching the road. We know he is prepared for this as he has binoculars. He sees an Aboriginal girl, Susan O'Connor, driving and she is the one fiddling with the radio. He chases her down and forces her to stop. He moves toward her as we see a long shot of how isolated they are. We see his face in her window looming above her and screaming about the electricity coming down from the mountains. This film is no murder mystery, as we know from the beginning that the murderer is Gregory the electrician. This is about the experiences of the other characters in the film and how they respond to current experiences.

The Kane family, Stewart, Claire and son Tom, is waking. Claire pretends to sleep, before waking suddenly and being affectionate with Tom. Stewart and Tom head out fishing. The scene doesn't feel quite right and there is some emotional tension between Stewart and Claire that is unspoken due to what they have experienced in the past. Claire had a complicated past when she was pregnant with Tom. When she finds she is pregnant again, she becomes emotional and slightly unstable.

As the film builds we see the complex pasts of the characters and their interactions in the confinement of the small town. The fishing trip is a break from this and extremely important in their lives.

We see some of the emotional instability in characters such as Caylin-Calandria, who with Tom, has some issues at school. Along with Caylin-Calandria, Claire and Jude also have issues but in a nicely framed shot of the three female characters, we see them conform as members of a close knit group. The sacrifice they make is similar to Gregory's but on a different scale. Note the connection here and how each one is to get back to order and societal norms. This is the collective experience for all the characters.

At the Kanes' home the tensions are obvious from their past experiences but they contain it for appearances' sake. Occasionally, the tension reaches breaking point and the experience strains the superficial approach. The tension builds at home and the fishing trip seems like a good opportunity to break the cycle.

When we see Gregory dump Susan O'Connor's body in the river, we know that the fishing and her death will interact.

The next morning, the fishermen head off for their one big trip of the year and the sign 'Gone fishing' is put in the garage window. We see Billy on the phone to Elissa and putting the sign the wrong way round in the window shows his immaturity. They have already said they are taking him away to make a man of him. The four men have a few beers on the way and talk as they travel through the landscape. They intend to give Billy the experience they think he needs as a 'man'—a cultural rite of passage.

The men arrive and the high-tension electricity wires punctuate the wilderness. They begin to hike toward the valley. It's a long walk in and the terrain is hilly and difficult. They stop on the way and again we see Billy's naivety when Stewart says 'Listen to that' meaning the silence but he can't, as he has his earphones in. It is part of the break in tension of the film that they commune with nature. This experiential break affects all the men. The episode represents a distinct human experience.

Stewart wanders down the river fishing and sees Susan's body caught in the rocks. Hesitantly, he wades out to it and turns it over saying 'Oh Jesus' repeatedly. He screams for the others to come as he drags the body to the bank. He is obviously upset, making the sign of the cross. Stewart tells Rocco to 'take her, for fuck's sake, take her' and their shock is obvious. They all stare at the body and Billy goes to run off but they stop him. The four men meet and decide to leave her in the water and tie her so she doesn't float away.

The presence of the body threatens to detract from the enjoyment of the fishing experience. The act of attempted isolation of the bad experience is expected to evoke only a mild response. They do not anticipate the stormy reaction it receives when they return to the community.

The men go on fishing, with Stewart getting the first big fish on an absolutely perfect day. The lure of the fish is strong, especially when they see the big one he has caught. They have a successful and enjoyable time, a positive experience. They get a photo of the catch and Billy holds up his fish in a typical hunter/gatherer pose. Capturing an experience this way is most enjoyable.

It is a photo that will come back to haunt them as things change back in the world. An unanticipated adverse reaction can be a horrific experience.

Stewart goes to check on the dead girl, rolling her over and getting debris off her face in a quite tender gesture. The next day they head back and report it. At the car Billy rings Elissa and says they found a body but 'caught the most amazing fish'. They are told by the police to wait and seem despondent their trip has been ruined. They organise their story as Stewart says they have 'to get their story straight'.

We cut to Gregory eating breakfast and he appears to be a normal, lonely man until he goes out to his shed where he has hidden Susan's car and this reminds us of the evil in him. Consider his experience and his motivations. How does he see his actions and the world?

The next day at the station the policeman tells the fishermen 'we don't step over bodies for our recreational pursuits' and 'the whole town's ashamed of you'. When they are told to 'piss off' from the station the press are waiting for them and Billy makes a comment. Carl is angry with the press but we can begin to see signs of distress within the whole group.

The experience they had so looked forward to has become a negative one and the tensions we saw before are exacerbated by the emotional and collective response to the murder. Claire soon becomes obsessed with the whole affair because of her own state. The newspaper the next day has the headline, 'Men fish over dead body' because Billy has talked. Billy is late to work and Stewart tells him they have to 'stick together on this'.

Susan's sister calls them 'animals' and raises the race question by asking if they would have left a white girl. The Aboriginal youths begin to attack and vandalise the property of the men in violent outbursts, including throwing a rock through Billy's van window and thus endangering his baby. They insult Carl at the caravan park and vandalise the garage.

The police aren't any help and the situation deteriorates. Jude tells the police they shouldn't be enforcing the 'political correctness' laws. The intervention of the sense of Aboriginality and race challenges the assumptions people have and how we see the world. The contrasting views are ingrained in the social structures and part of different collective experiences.

The Aboriginal people see the white people as 'interfering' and the group of fishermen begin to fight amongst themselves. Elissa says they shouldn't go to the bush at all as it's sacred. The group talk about the bush and Rocco punches Stewart for saying the Aborigines are superstitious. The experience of racial tension becomes ever-present and adds to the emotional responses to the experience.

We now head slowly to a resolution of the conflict brought about by the various experiences. Each is handled in a different manner by characters and you can explore one or two of the responses. To cycle back to the original murder, Claire is stalked by Gregory in his truck. He stops her but drives off after staring weirdly, an odd experience in itself.

Terry and Stewart talk and Stewart meets Rocco and Carl. He tells them Claire's left him 'again'. Rocco can't believe it and we cross cut to her looking out into the wilderness after he looks thoughtfully out the window. These different reactions to experiences mirror attitudes in life and reactions to emotional and intellectual conflict.

In conclusion, Lawrence takes us back to the healing power of nature in our human experiences when the Aboriginal people are having a ceremony. Gregory watches while Claire walks in. Again we see his truck as an omnipresent force in the film, almost an extension of him. An Aboriginal man tells Claire to 'piss off' from the ceremony after she says she has come to pay her 'respects' but he is told to leave her alone by an Auntie.

The smoke and tribal music symbolise the ceremonial nature of the setting and the camera pans around the scene and the bush. We see parts of the ceremony with chanting and clapping sticks. The camera moves in and out while other shots pan around the bush, giving us the full experience and Lawrence portrays this as a positive, healing experience.

Eventually Stewart, Tom, Carl, Jude and Rocco arrive to pay respects. Tom runs to his mother and Stewart goes over and says 'Sorry' but is rebuffed by the father who throws dirt on him and spits, refusing his apology. Then an Aboriginal girl tells a little about Susan's story and sings the last love song Susan wrote.

The camera pans around all the faces as they listen to the song and the ceremonial smoke wafts around. It seems to have some healing effect on everyone, as it is a meaningful experience which raises the idea of the spiritual experience in the text. The girl stops singing through emotion. 'Be gone' seems to symbolise in language the whole scenario for each character.

We see a long wide shot of the bush before fading back to Gregory waiting again in his car behind the rocks for another victim. It is quite a circular conclusion and it is an odd end when he crushes the fly. We don't quite know what to make of the whole experience and he seems to be the only character unchanged by the experiences in the film.

Poem: 'Inland' by John Kinsella

The poem captures the mood and ethos of the outback farming communities and deals with the human aspect more than some of the other poems in Kinsella's collection: *Peripheral Light*. This poem is one long restless thought that mimics memories and recollection while raising the current, topical issues that concern the poet. As usual with his poems Kinsella orientates the audience early with the word 'Inland' and then continues the poem without a full stop. The poem flows with the use of commas but Kinsella allows us to stop and think with the use of the colon, brackets and the hyphen. Look for these punctuation stops as you read as they emphasise a specific point or idea that resonates with the audience.

The first stanza gives us a foreshadowing of the events to follow with the warnings in the words 'storm', 'alert' and 'uncertain'. This ominous tone is reinforced by the word 'ghosts' and the implication of death which is constant in much of Kinsella's poetry. The next stanza deals with a more human element and we get the country feel with the bracketed gossip about McHenry's accident which shows the close knit community. Habits here are formed as part of survival and known to all as we see 'the old man plying the same track' and the families possibly heading to church on the Sunday morning.

The third stanza returns to the vagaries of nature. Kinsella repeats 'uncertain' with regard to the weather. Weather and the environment play a large role in farming communities and it is especially so at sowing and harvest. Despite the uncertainty and 'ashen' days which alter 'moods', the community returns to their habits and routines which shape their lives. The next stage returns to the road and the implication of a journey but a journey that is straight and in conflict with the cycles of the natural world. The path seems already marked and measured. It is 'straight and narrow', marked by a theodolite.

The final four lines of the poem are pure Kinsella, marking the transience of humanity on the landscape. We read

> 'it's a place of borrowed dreams
> where the marks of the spirit
> have been erased by dust –
> the restless topsoil'

The European farmers had 'borrowed dreams' for their own relationship with the land but this line also harks back to the indigenous Dreamtime when the land was created. The indigenous view that the land owns the people is also true for Kinsella. This sense of nobody owning the land is strong in his poetry. European impact on the land can be seen in the spirituality being removed by the dust—dust created by the poor farming techniques transferred from a different land. He finishes with the 'restless topsoil' as if the whole earth is moving in its own discontented journey, just as the people move.

The influence here of genuinely lost spirituality and connection with the land as we move directly on the 'high road' contrasts with the more flowing, 'restless' side of the natural world. This visual contrast is obvious but we can also discuss the contrast between habit and spirit. 'Inland' is a poem that uses the landscape to show the contrast between two views of the countryside.

DRAMA: Eugene O'Neil's *Desire Under the Elms*

O'Neill sets out to instruct how the house and elms should appear and the year is 1850. Note how he describes the 'enormous' elms as,

> 'exhausted women resting their sagging breasts and hands and hair on its roof, and when it rains their tears trickle down monotonously and rot on the shingles'

and how they dominate and 'rot'. It is important to read this both in terms of the play and in the context of American theatre. The description here shows O'Neill's genius at new design and original theatricality.

Part One: Scene One

The whole first page and a third are nearly all playwright notes that describe the farm, the house and the characters of Eben, Simeon and Peter. The first words of the play, 'God! Purty!' reflect the beauty of the land and how Eben perceives it. Eben is 'resentful and defensive' and feels 'trapped' on the farm.

His older half-brothers Simeon and Peter are 'more bounce and homelier in face, shrewder and more practical.' They all have worked hard on their father's farm over the years and have little feeling for their absent father. We learn that Simeon had a 'woman' who died and that Peter is excited by the prospect of 'gold in the West'. They all talk about how hard they've worked and hope that the father might 'die soon'. What we get from all this is that they are earthy and this is reflected in their bodies and clothes which are all dirt stained.

We also see here the difference between them as Eben sees gold in the pasture, not California, as they head in for a dinner of bacon in what seems a ritual they have performed many times before. Note that O'Neill calls for the use of the curtain at the end of the scene.

Scene Two

It is twilight and again we get detailed notes on the interior scene. Simeon tells Eben he should not wish their father dead and Eben replies he's not his son but, 'I'm Maw – every drop of blood!' He then blames the father, Ephraim Cabot, for killing his mother by working her to death but the others just say there was work to be done. O'Neill gets them to list the jobs and Eben comes back with 'vengeful passion' that, while they did nothing, he will see his mother gets 'rest and sleep in her grave!'

They then discuss Cabot's absence and how he just drove off in a buggy one day in a rush. Simeon says that when he went,

> 'He druv off in the buggy, all spick an' span, with the mare all breshed an' shiny, druv off clackin' his tongue an' wavin' his whip. I remember it quite well'

Eben mocks Simeon for not stopping him and the scene concludes with Eben leaving to see Minnie the town whore. We learn all the Cabot men have slept with her. Simeon and Peter say that Eben is just like 'Paw' and thinks of California. The final image is of Eben with his arms stretched to the sky talking about starts and sin, 'my sin's as purty as any one on 'em!', until he 'strides' to the village for Min.

Scene Three

It is 'pitch darkness' and Eben comes home with the news that Cabot has married a 'purty' thirty-five year old. He has heard this in the village and this effectively disinherits the boys. Simeon and Peter see California as their only option now. Eben tells the boys that they can have three hundred dollars each if they sign their share of the farm over to him. He can get the money as his mother told him,

> 'I know whar it's hid. I been waitin' – Maw told me. She knew whar it lay fur years, but she was waitin'....It's her'n – the money he hoarded from her farm an' hid from Maw. It's my money by rights now.'

They think about it and Eben tells them about his night with Min. He tells how he hates the new wife after the boys suggest he might sleep with her, just like Min, to get the old man back. Peter and Simeon say they'll do the deal and leave the farm. Both are bitter and vindictive about Cabot.

Scene Four

The setting is the same as Scene Two and the boys are discussing how they don't have to work now – it is all down to Eben who is jubilant as he thinks it will all be his. Peter and Simeon again reflect on how like his father he is, 'Like his Paw'. They also tell he isn't much of a milker but they soon talk about their leaving and how they'll miss some aspects of the farm.

Eben comes back in and says that the 'old mule an the bride' are coming. The two older boys begin to pack and sign Eben's papers as he gives them the money Cabot had hidden. They tell him they'll send him 'a lump o' gold for Christmas' and head into the yard feeling 'light' because of their newfound freedom.

Ephraim Cabot and Abbie Putnam then come in and O'Neill describes them in detail. Cabot is

> 'seventy-five, tall and gaunt, with great, wiry, concentrated power, but stoop shouldered by toil. His face is hard as if it were hewn from a boulder, yet there is a weakness in it'

but his face is weakened with petty pride. Abbie is

> 'thirty-five, buxom, full of vitality. Her round face is pretty but marred by its rather gross sensuality. There is strength and obstinacy in her jaw, a hard determination in her eyes, and about her whole personality.'

She also has a 'desperate quality'. Cabot shows Abbie the place and she says to him it's 'mine'. Then he sees the two boys not working. He introduces Abbie and she goes to look at 'her' house and they warn her Eben's inside.

Cabot tells them to get to work and they give him cheek, saying they are 'free' and heading to California. They 'whoop' it up and he says he'll have them chained up. They throw rocks at the house, smashing the window and head off singing. Abbie sticks her head out the window and says she likes the room but he is thinking of the stock and 'almost runs' to the barn.

Abbie then meets Eben in the kitchen and talks to him in 'seductive tones'. She says she doesn't want to be his 'Maw' but friends and he cusses her. She tells him of her troubled life and how Cabot gave her a chance to escape it. He calls her a 'harlot' and they argue over ownership of the farm. She has the upper hand in law and he leaves but the seeds of their growing attraction have been set.

Outside he and his father argue about life and work and he tells Eben 'Ye'll never be more'n half a man!' The scene ends with Abbie washing up and the faint notes of the song the boys were singing as they left.

Part Two: Scene One

Again O'Neill describes in detail the farmhouse setting. Two months have passed and it is a hot Sunday afternoon. Abbie in her best outfit is sitting on the porch and Eben comes out of the house also dressed in his best. They stalk each other, both attracted and repelled. As he walks away she 'gives a sneering, taunting chuckle' at him and they argue but the attraction is obvious. She says that nature will pull him to her but he says that she is married and he goes to leave her.

She accuses him of going to Min and she gets angry stating he'll never get the farm,

> 'Ye'll never live t' see the day when even a stinkin' weed on it 'll belong t' ye!'

He says he hates her and leaves as Cabot enters. She tells him Eben has been mocking him and twists the conversation to the inheritance of the farm. She tells him Eben lusts after her and as he angers she backs off in her accusations. Reassured, he says that she can have the farm if she bears the son she says she wants with him. He says that he'd 'do anythin' ye axed, I tell ye!' if she gave him a son and tells her to pray to God for it to happen.

Scene Two

It is about eight in the evening and here the bedrooms are highlighted, with Eben in one and Cabot with Abbie in the other. The two of them are talking about a son. They seem together, yet apart, as he tells her of his life on the farm and how God's hard. He both lost and gained on the way through, but the farm is his. He says he is pleased he found her, his 'Rose o' Sharon'. Abbie promises him that she will bear a son as he basically threatens her,

> 'Ye don't know nothin' – nor never will. If ye don't hev a son t' redeem ye...'

and he leaves to sleep in the barn with the cows 'whar it's restful'.

We then see Eben and Abbie restless and she leaves the room and goes to him. He 'submits' to her kisses then 'hurls' her away. Abbie says she'd make him 'happy' and she knows he wants her too much. She tells him to go down to the parlour and he is shocked as this is where his mother was 'laid out'. She leaves for the parlour and he wonders what's happening. The scene closes with a question to his dead mother, 'Maw! Whar are yew?' but we know that he wants her and will go to her.

Scene Three

The scene now shifts to the parlour which is described as a 'grim, repressed room like a tomb'. Abbie waits and Eben appears and he sits at her invitation. They talk about his Maw and how they hate Cabot. Abbie throws herself at him with 'wild passion' and he is caught up in the moment and thinks that it's his Maw wanting him to sleep with Abbie to get revenge on Cabot,

> I see it! I sees why. It's her vengeance on him – so's she kin rest quiet in her grave!

Abbie proclaims her love for him and he for her then they kiss 'in a fierce, bruising kiss' to close the scene.

Scene Four

A more bold and confident Eben leaves the house and Abbie opens the parlour window. She calls him over for a kiss and they talk a bit before Eben says his Maw can now rest. They split as Cabot comes out of the barn but are now obviously in love. Eben tells Cabot that his Maw is now at rest and Cabot says he rests best with the cows. Cabot is confused but the scene ends with him criticising Eben as 'Soft-headed' and a 'born fool' but, being a practical man, he heads for breakfast.

Part Three: Scene One

Time has passed to 'late spring the following year'. Eben is upstairs in emotional and psychological conflict while a party happens downstairs. Cabot has drunk too much and Abbie sits, pale and thin, in a rocking chair. There is a fiddler and Abbie begins the scene by asking for Eben and the guests 'titter' as most think the baby is Eben's, not Cabot's, which is true enough. They laugh and Cabot is angered by this and orders them to dance. The fiddler 'slyly' says they're waiting for Eben but Cabot mocks the boy and then ensues a bawdy conversation about his fertility,

> I got a lot in me – a hell of a lot – folks don't know on. Fiddle 'er up, durn ye! Give 'em somethin' t' dance t!'

The fiddler plays and they dance. Cabot joins in frantically and 'whoop(s)' it up. He exhausts the fiddler and pours whiskey. In the upstairs room Eben is looking at the baby. Abbie goes upstairs and Cabot leaves for outside, 'fresh air', as she has told him not to 'tech' her. The guests gossip after he goes and we see Eben and Abbie upstairs and she professes her love for him,

> 'Don't git feelin' low. I love ye, Eben. Kiss me.'

Cabot says he's going to rest in the barn. The scene concludes with the fiddler playing in celebration of 'the old skunk gittin' fooled!'

Scene Two

Eben is outside half an hour later and Cabot is coming back from the barn. Cabot tells him to get a woman inside and he might get a farm. Eben replies that this farm's his and Cabot mocks him. He tells her Abbie has been promised the farm for her son and Eben is angered thinking Abbie has tricked him.

Eben goes to kill her but Cabot is too strong for him and Abbie comes out to stop him choking Eben. Cabot tells him he's weak and goes inside to celebrate. Abbie tries to be tender with Eben but he rejects her and calls her a liar.

> 'Ye're nothin' but a stinkin' passel o' lies. Ye've been lyin' t' me every word ye spoke, day an' night, since we fust – done it. Ye've kept sayin' ye loved me....'

She says she loves him and tells him that the promise was made before they fell in love. He says he'll go to California.

They argue and he 'torturedly' says he wished the baby had never been born. Abbie is distraught and she says she'd kill the baby to prove her love for him. He says he won't listen to her but she calls after him that she can 'prove' she loves him and she 'kin do one thin' God does'. Abbie is desperate at the end of the scene.

Scene Three

It is now just before dawn and Eben is in the kitchen ready to leave. Abbie is near the cradle with 'her face full of terror'. She sobs but Cabot stirs and she goes to the kitchen and flings her arms around Eben, kissing him 'wildly'. She says 'I killed him' and he thinks she means Cabot but is horrified when she tells him it's the baby.

Eben states it was his baby and she says she loved it but loves him more. He is angered,

> 'Don't ye tech me! Ye're pizzen! How could ye – t' murder
> a pore little critter – Ye must've swapped yer soul t' hell!

and tells her that he is getting the Sheriff and heads, 'panting and sobbing' to town. She calls out to him that she loves him.

Scene Four

It is after dawn and Abbie is in the kitchen. Cabot wakes in his room and is concerned that he has woken late. He checks the baby and is proud it is quiet and asleep. He goes down to Abbie in the kitchen and she tells him the baby is dead. He runs to check and comes back down and asks 'why?'

In a rage she tells him it was Eben's son and that she loves Eben, not him. He blinks back a tear and then gets 'stony' so he can carry on and says he is going to get the Sheriff. Abbie tells him that Eben's already gone so that Cabot tells her he'll 'git t' wuk.' He then tells her he'd never have told and now he's going to be 'lonesomer'n ever!' Eben comes back and Cabot tells him to get off the farm.

Eben asks for her forgiveness and tells her he loves her. He says he realised he loved her at the Sheriff's and they have a chance to run away but Abbie says she'll take her punishment. Eben says he will share it with her and plans to tell the Sheriff they planned it together. They think they can stand it together and then Cabot comes back.

He goes into a long tirade and tells them how he's let the stock go and will burn the house down. He too plans to go to California but finds that Eben has gotten to his money first. Cabot says that this is a sign from God to him to stay and that 'God's hard an' lonesome!' At this point the Sheriff comes and Eben says he was involved with the baby's murder.

Cabot says 'Take 'em both' and leaves to get his stock. The sun is coming up and as they are led away Eben says the farm's 'Purty' and Abbie agrees. The Sheriff finishes the play with the line, 'It's a jim-dandy farm, no denyin'. Wish I owned it!'

OTHER RELATED TEXTS

Fiction / Non-fiction / Drama

- *Wonder* – R G Palacio
- *First they Killed My Father* – Luong Ung
- *The Graveyard Book* – Neil Gaiman
- *Looking for Alaska* – John Green
- *Eleanor and Park* by Rainbow Rowell
- *The Fault in Our Stars* – John Green
- *We All Fall Down* – Robert Cormier
- *The Old Man and the Sea* – Ernest Hemingway
- *The Fire Eaters* – David Almond
- *Ender's Game* – Orson Scott Card
- *Hatchet* – Gary Paulsen
- *Inside Black Australia* – Kevin Gilbert
- *Sapiens: A Brief History of Humankind* – Yuval Noah Harari
- *Peeling the Onion* – Wendy Orr
- *Raw* – Scott Monk
- *Six Degrees of Separation* – John Guare
- *The Book Thief* – Markus Zusak
- *When Dogs Cry* – Markus Zusak
- *Holes* – Louis Sachar
- *The Outsiders* – S.E. Hinton
- *Roll of Thunder, Hear My Cry* – Mildred D. Taylor
- *A Small Free Kiss in the Dark* – Glenda Millard
- *Monster* – Walter Dean Myers
- *Lord of the Flies* – William Golding
- *Jandamarra* – Steve Hawke
- *A Separate Peace* – John Knowles
- *A Monster Calls* – Patrick Ness
- *The Pigman* – Paul Zindel
- *The Invention of Hugo Cabret* – Brian Selznik

- *Emerald City* – David Williamson
- *Silent Spring* – Rachel Carson

Films and Television

- *The Human Experience* – Charles Kinnane
- *My Brilliant Career* – Gillian Armstrong
- *Broadchurch* – James Strong & Euros Lyn
- *Twinsters* – Samantha Futerman and Ryan Miyamoto
- *Be My Brother* – Genevieve Clay - Smith
- *What's Eating Gilbert Grape* – Lasse Hallstrom
- *Pleasantville* – Gary Ross
- *Eternal Sunshine of the Spotless Mind* – Michel Gondry
- *Taxi Driver* – Martin Scorsese
- *Tootsie* – Sydney Pollack
- *Back in Time for Dinner* – Kim Maddever
- *The Godfather* – Francis Ford Coppola
- *Friends* – David Crane and Marta Kaufmann
- *Dawson's Creek* – Kevin Williamson
- *Orange is the New Black* – Jenji Kohan
- *Boy Meets World* – Michael Jacobs and April Kelly

Website – quote on literature and the human experience

http://view2.fdu.edu/academics/university-college/school-of-humanities/english-language-and-literature-program/

> At its most fundamental level literature explores what it means to be a human being in this world and tries to describe what our human experience is like. As such, literature pushes us to confront the large human questions that have plagued humankind for centuries: issues of fate and free will, issues relating to our role in the universe, our relationship to God, and our

relationships with others. Studying literature not only helps us to understand the complexity of these questions intellectually, but because of its very nature, it allows us to experience these tensions vicariously. Literature does not just tell us about human experience; it recreates it in a way we can feel and visualise. In other words, it calls for a total response from us—it stretches us beyond who we are.

First, literature can enhance our ability to relate to people. Because literature focuses on human relationships and self perception, it can broaden our own experience—to help us understand different kinds of people, different cultures, different problems—and, consequently, help us better understand our own relationships with others.

The study of literature also helps to foster an appreciation for beauty, symmetry, and order. This means more than the intuitive response of liking or disliking something we see or read or hear; it means a carefully thought-through response that will enhance appreciation—not destroy it.

Perhaps the most important skills that the study of literature teaches are analytic and synthetic skills. In learning to read carefully and analytically, we learn to ask hard questions both of the work and of ourselves. And as we seek to discover the relationships between the ideas and images we uncover in a work, our ultimate goal is to see the whole—to see how the parts work together to make the piece what it is. In grappling with the complex and difficult ideas contained in literature, we learn to accept the multiple dimensions and ambiguity that are so often present in life.

Finally, the study of literature will also help develop our writing abilities as we come to value the written word and understand its power to communicate.

Beyond all of these skills, however, it is not what literature can do for us as individuals as much as what it can do to us. Literature speaks to the whole person. Listen to it, says C. S. Lewis, and you will be changed.

Poetry

- 'Warren Pryor' – Alden Nowlan
- 'The Gardener' – Louis MacNeice
- 'The Improvers' – Colin Thiele

Songs

- *Be My Escape* – Relient K
- *Mandolin Wind* – Rod Stewart
- *Roxanne* – The Police
- *Wake Me Up When September Ends* – Green Day
- *Under Pressure* – Queen & David Bowie
- *Candle in the Wind* – Elton John
- *Empire State of Mind* – Alicia Keys
- *Gold Digger* – Kanye West
- *We Are Young* – Fun.
- *Centrefold* – J. Geils Band
- *It's Time* – Imagine Dragons
- *We Cry* – The Script
- *If I Were a Boy* – Beyoncé
- *Shake it Out* – Florence + the Machine
- *C'mon* – Panic! At the Disco & Fun.
- *I Don't Love You* – My Chemical Romance
- *Sing* – My Chemical Romance
- *1985* – Bowling for Soup
- *What About Me* – Shannon Noll
- *Sinner* – Jeremy Loops
- *7 Years* – Lucas Graham

- *Bitter Sweet Symphony* – The Verve
- *Ghost!* – Kid Kudi
- *Good Riddance (Time of Your Life)* – Green Day
- *Expectations* – Belle and Sebastian
- *After Hours* – We Are Scientists
- *Write About Love* – Belle and Sebastian
- *Trust Your Stomach* – Marching Band
- *Heaven Knows I'm Miserable Now* – The Smiths